ONE WEST 54TH STREET FOUNDATION

June 2015

Dear University Club Member

It is with great pleasure that we enclose your copy of *The University Club, 1865-2015*. This beautiful, informative, and entertaining volume will be a fine addition to your collection. It will also provide—for years to come—a marvelous reminder of the "life and times" of The University Club, from its tentative start as a small group of young university men seeking to extend the camaraderie of their college days, to the present day, when the men and women who constitute our membership have made the Club one of the most respected social institutions not only in New York, but also in the nation and beyond.

Your donation to the One West 54th Street Foundation has helped to fund the creation and publication of this fine volume. It will also help the Foundation to continue the fine work it does in insuring that the façade of our extraordinary clubhouse is cared for in a way that will allow this splendid structure to be passed along to future generations of members, and to future generations of New Yorkers, to whom it is a treasured landmark.

We hope that you will enjoy—as we have—perusing this fine volume.

Sincerely,

John E. Osnato
President
One West 54th Street Foundation

Paul N. Leitner
President
The University Club

ONE WEST 54TH STREET
NEW YORK, NEW YORK 10019
212-572-3400

Library of Congress Cataloging-in-Publication Data

The University Club, 1865–2015 / edited by Percy Preston Jr.

pages cm

Includes bibliographical references.

ISBN 978-1-57864-962-4 (hard cover : alk. paper)

1. University Club (New York, N.Y.) 2. Private clubs—New York (State)—New
York—History. I. Preston, Percy, Jr.

HS2725.N5U629 2015

367'.97471—dc23

2015003729

Published by The Donning Company Publishers, Virginia Beach, Virginia, and printed in
the United States of America at Walsworth Publishing Company, Marceline, Missouri

TABLE OF CONTENTS

FOREWORD

In our Sesquicentennial year, The University Club enjoys membership at capacity, a waiting list for admission and a very engaged clubhouse and staff.

We must be grateful to those who preceded us, who led the Club through many recessions and depressions, several wars, and times of social unrest. Through it all, The University Club has served as a beacon of comfort and tradition. It has proven to be an oasis of serenity to its members and their guests, against the backdrop of a dynamic but sometimes frenetic New York.

Vibrant activity throughout the Club stems from outstanding member committee leadership. Their inspiration and creativity make it possible for the Club to host multiple, diverse events daily throughout the year. Their efforts are supported by club management and staff who continue to set the tone of professionalism and esprit de corps that is contagious throughout the clubhouse.

As we commemorate the 150th anniversary of our founding, we take pride in and salute our founders and those who followed, sustaining the Club's rich history and traditions. We celebrate our Sesquicentennial and hope this volume preserves some of that pride we all possess.

Paul N. Leitner
President

PREFACE

On behalf of the Library and Art Committee, welcome to this wonderful moment in the 150 years of the life of The University Club. This sesquicentennial volume pays tribute to the Club's social and architectural history, its décor, its library, and the many and varied passions of our membership.

Consistent with the Club's culture of service and cooperation, this book is the product of Club members and Club staff, and would not have been able to see the light of day without the steerage of four key contributors: former Library and Art Committee Chair Percy Preston Jr., who has led the project from inception, former Library and Art Committee member Ben Steinberg, who has acted as Editor, Club General Manager John Dorman, and Library Director and Curator of Collections Andrew Berner, and his Library staff.

It is with great pleasure that The University Club

Library and its Committee have overseen the publication of this sesquicentennial review of 150 years of Club life. As stipulated in The University Club Charter, the Library and Art Collections are central to our Club, and today, thanks to the tremendous efforts by all Club committees, we can see how the Club has developed since 1865 to embrace the desires and diverse interests of our membership. Warm hospitality is offered to members and guests alike in our dining rooms and overnight accommodations, cultural interests are cultivated, athleticism is prized, the voices of all generations of our membership drive continued enrichment of our activities. We acknowledge the leadership demonstrated by our 20th and 21st century presidents, and extend our thanks to President Paul N. Leitner for his strong encouragement and support for this effort, and to former President John Osnato and the One West 54th Street Foundation for its interest in this sesquicentennial album.

ΕΝ ΚΟΙΝΩΝΙΑΙ Η ΦΙΛΙΑ

"In Fellowship Lies Friendship"

With gratitude,
C. Casey Bayles
Chair, Library and Art Committee

INTRODUCTION

In early summer 2012, Paul N. Leitner, then newly elected president of the Club, asked if the Library and Art Committee, of which I was then chairman, would accept the responsibility of preparing a "coffee table" book to commemorate the Club's sesquicentennial three years hence. The Committee agreed to do so, and this book is the result.

The history of The University Club has been written on two occasions, by James Alexander in *A History of The University Club of New York, 1865–1915* (1915), and by Guy St. Clair, in *A Venerable and Cherished Institution* (1991). In 1955, the Club published *The University Club, Yesterday and Today*, with a number of charming stories edited by William L. Chenery. This book contained a series of sketches of parts of the clubhouse by Robert Ball that today are hanging in the corridor leading to the manager's office. The clubhouse centennial in 1999 was observed with the publishing of a book of photographs of the building. In addition, there have been specialized volumes covering the Library ceiling, the art collection and presidents of the Club.

Although the present volume does not repeat all the data found in the Alexander and St. Clair histories, it does owe a debt to both the earlier authors. Without their exhaustive research into the Club, the task of the present authors would have been much more time-consuming.

The Club archives contain a collection of scrapbooks reaching from the late 19th century through the 1980s. For decades, it was the custom to place a copy of every invitation, announcement, letter and report sent to the membership in these books. The books also include menus, seating charts for grand dinners, photographs, press clippings, exhibition catalogues and the texts of speeches given on special occasions. A selection of these items have been scanned and appear in the "Club Life" chapter, to convey, with a light touch, a sense of how members made use of their Club, what they ate, who came to speak here, and how the Club perceived itself within the context of the city and country.

As the Club moved in the direction of electronic communication, the practice of keeping scrapbooks was discontinued. For the last two decades, therefore, the book relies on a narrower selection of visual materials to convey a sense of life within the walls of the clubhouse.

Interwoven with the illustrations are short pieces covering the founding of the Club in 1865, its rebirth in 1879, and the effects of two world wars, Prohibition and the Great Depression on the Club. Another piece describes the process through which women gained full participation in the Club. The reader will also find chapters devoted to the Library, squash, fitness, fine arts and decorative arts. Furthermore, each standing and informal committee wrote about its activities.

This book is the work of many hands. Each of the people who contributed articles merits our deep gratitude.

In addition, thanks are due to:

Benjamin Steinberg, who edited the entire volume. Its literary quality was enhanced as a result.

Christopher Serbagi and his colleague David Marcus, who devoted countless hours to tracing the copyright owners of illustrations, and to obtaining the consent of various prominent people for their images to appear in the book.

Scott Overall, who patiently instructed me in the operation of the high-tech scanner in the Library Office and came to my rescue whenever the machine proved recalcitrant.

In addition to writing about the Library and its rare book collection with his customary passion, Andrew Berner gathered many of the illustrations of the building and helped in ways large and small throughout the whole process.

John Dorman's many contributions to the book project include identifying Lee Dunnette as the right person to prepare the splendid rendering of the clubhouse, and working with him as the illustration took shape. He also obtained permission for our photographer to access a building on the east side of Fifth Avenue, oversaw the marketing effort, and was instrumental in shepherding the production process forward on schedule.

Lars Dewenter, front office manager, devoted a Saturday morning in August to helping our photographer, Jon Wallen, obtain the cover photograph.

Michael Foss, who has devoted countless hours searching in archives around the city for images of the clubhouse, found the photograph which includes the former roof garden.

Sabrina Funk, whose skills and good taste are familiar to Club members through *The Illuminator*, designed the book. She and I spent countless hours on the telephone discussing placement of illustrations, their captions, the organization of the book, and myriad other details.

To my former colleagues on the Library and Art Committee, who may not have realized what they were getting themselves into, thanks for your support and for permitting me to carry this project forward.

Percy Preston Jr.

I

HUMBLE BEGINNINGS

by Percy Preston Jr.

The month of April 1865 is remembered for several momentous events. On the 9th, Robert E. Lee surrendered to Ulysses S. Grant at Appomattox Court House in Virginia. On the 14th, Abraham Lincoln was shot in Ford's Theater. In that context, the passage of Chapter 594 of the Laws of 1865 by the New York State Legislature on the 28th would seem but a small footnote. Yet it is that footnote that concerns us, for Chapter 594 is entitled "An Act to Incorporate The University Club in the City of New York." That act serves as the legal foundation for the Club to this day.

The genesis of the Club may be traced to 1861, when a group of recent Yale College graduates started to meet informally on Saturday evenings to play whist in the townhouse of Joseph Kernochan, located at 145 Second Avenue. As the décor of the room in which the group gathered was red, they gave themselves the name "Red Room Club." One of the group was Henry Holt, later a prominent publisher, who wrote a memorandum about the early years of the Club, now the source for much of our knowledge of its early history.

In 1864, when illness in the Kernochan family made it impossible to continue meeting at their house, the

The first clubhouse at 9 Brevoort Place

group met for a time at the Holt household at 7 West 30th Street. When Holt and his wife made plans to be away from the city for some time, thereby depriving the group of a place to meet, someone offered the suggestion, "We must found a University Club." As many of the young men had gone on to study at Columbia Law School, they held the organization meeting in the law school, then located at University Place. Professor Theodore W. Dwight had taught most of the young

Henry Holt

men at law school, and he accepted their offer to be the first president of the new Club. The statute listed thirteen men who founded the Club, five of whom were Yale graduates, two from Harvard, two from Columbia and one each from Hamilton, NYU, Göttingen (Germany), and CCNY.

The new Club started with a burst of enthusiasm, and there were soon 112 members on the rolls. They rented a furnished house at 9 Brevoort Place (now East 10th Street between Broadway and University Place) for $5,000 per year. However, financial problems soon arose as, in Henry Holt's words, "its original members were too young and obscure," and without club experience.

Theodore W. Dwight

One who was neither young nor obscure was George Templeton Strong, a prominent lawyer best remembered today as the author of a celebrated diary. Strong, who graduated from Columbia College in 1838, was presumably responsible for shepherding the application through the legislature.

With the rent in arrears, by November 1865 Professor Dwight was obliged to send a dunning letter pointing out that less than half the members had

The new Club started with a burst of enthusiasm, and there were soon 112 members on the rolls. They rented a furnished house at 9 Brevoort Place for $5,000 per year.

paid their dues and fees. In the autumn of 1867, the Brevoort Place house was vacated and the landlady given a note for the unpaid rent (whether the note was ever satisfied is unclear). With the Club homeless, most members drifted away. Professor Dwight stepped aside, and George Van Nest Baldwin was elected president at a meeting held at a member's house. He would hold office for twelve years, until 1879. During this period of desuetude, the Club's charter would be kept alive through informal meetings in private houses.

George Van Nest Baldwin

An Act
To incorporate "the University
Club" in the city of New York.

The People of the State of New York, represented in Senate and Assembly, do enact as follows:

Section 1. Theodore Woolsey Dwight, George T. Strong, John Taylor Johnston, Charles Astor Bristed, Henry R. Winthrop, Charles L. Chandler, Joseph H. Choate, Edward Wetmore, Francis E. Kernochan, Eugene Schuyler, Edward Mitchell, Luther M. Jones and Russell Sturgis jr. and such other persons as are now associated or may hereafter be associated with them, are hereby constituted a body corporate by the name of "The University Club", to be located in the city of New York, for the purpose of the promotion of literature and art, by establishing and maintaining a library, reading room and gallery of art, and by such other means as shall be expedient and proper for such purpose.

§2. The said Corporation shall have the power to make and adopt a constitution and by-laws, rules and regulations for the admission, suspension and expulsion of its members, and for their government, for the collection of fees and dues, for the election of its officers, and to define their duties, and for the safe keeping and protection of its property and funds, and from time to time to alter or repeal such constitution, by-laws, rules and regulations. The persons named in the first section of this act shall constitute the trustees and managers until others are elected in their places.

§3. The said corporation may lease, purchase or take by deed, devise or bequest, any real or personal estate, and hold or lease the same; provided that they shall not hold any real estate the value of which shall exceed the sum of one hundred thousand dollars.

§4. The said Corporation shall possess the general powers and be subject to the general restrictions and liabilities prescribed in the third title of the eighteenth chapter of the first part of the Revised Statutes.

§5. This act shall take effect immediately.

State of New York

In Assembly April 24. 1865

This bill was read the third time and passed, a majority of all the Members elected, voting in favor thereof

By order of the Assembly

G G Hoskins Speaker.

State of New York.

In Senate. March 11 1865.

This bill was read the third time and passed, a majority of all the Senators elected voting in favor thereof.

By order of the Senate.

Thomas G. Alvord President

Approved April 28th 1865

R E Fenton

The original text of Chapter 594, Laws of New York, 1865, signed by Gov. Reuben Fenton

II

REBIRTH AND RENEWAL

by Percy Preston Jr.

By the late 1870s, the climate for starting an institution was more propitious, as the effects of the Panic of 1873 had mostly worn off and the city was enjoying the flood tide of post-Civil War prosperity. In Henry Holt's words, "By the time many of the young men of the Club of 1865 had attained wealth and position, club life had made wonderful progress in New York…" The nucleus of members had little difficulty in recruiting several hundred men interested in a revived Club. In March 1879, there was an organizational meeting held at Delmonico's restaurant at Fifth Avenue and 26th Street, by which time the rolls of the Club had swelled to 502 members. In May, at another meeting, the membership elected twenty men to the Council, divided into four classes of five each, and twenty-one members to the Committee on Admissions, divided into three classes of seven each. The executive authority to operate the Club was vested in the Council, with the Committee on Admissions having exclusive power to admit members. At a Council meeting four days later, the Council classified itself and the Admissions Committee by lot to determine who would be in which class. They also elected new officers. Henry Anderson became president, and George Van Nest Baldwin became vice president once more. Thus the structure of governance familiar to Club members today was established.

The second clubhouse, Fifth Avenue and 35th Street

The next priority was to find a clubhouse, and the Council settled on a (then-vacant) house at the corner of Fifth Avenue and 35th Street, which was rented for a period of five years at an annual rental of $9,000. This house had space for a library, a dining room and a billiard room.

As the Club gained members, this facility became too small, and in 1884, the Club moved into the former Jerome mansion on Madison Avenue and 26th Street. The builder of this place was the maternal grandfather of Winston S. Churchill, a Wall Street speculator named Leonard Jerome. After the Jerome family vacated the house, it was used by two other clubs prior to being

The third clubhouse, the former Leonard Jerome mansion, Madison Avenue and 26th Street

JOHN W. ALEXANDER (1856–1915)
James W. Alexander, 1893

Oil on canvas,
50 x 35 inches

James W. Alexander was president of the Club from 1891 to 1899. He was a guiding force behind the decision to enlarge the membership and move to a new location. Alexander served on the committee that acquired the land at 54th Street and Fifth Avenue for the new clubhouse, and had a role in selecting Charles McKim as the architect. After stepping down from the presidency, he served on the Council and on the Committee on Literature and Art. Alexander is the author of *A History of The University Club of New York 1865-1915* (1915). The Alexander Fund in the Club's endowment is named in his honor.

JOHN W. ALEXANDER (1856–1915)
Dr. David L. Haight, 1899

Oil on canvas,
39½ x 29¼ inches

David L. Haight was chairman of the House Committee from 1891 to 1902 and served on the Committee on Plans and Building that oversaw the construction of the clubhouse. So numerous were his contributions to the Club, and so high the esteem in which he was held, that in 1896, the Council voted to award him "the free hospitalities of the club," and henceforth he was a guest. Haight is the only House Committee chairman (other than those who were subsequently president of the Club) to have his portrait hung in the clubhouse.

leased to The University Club for $22,500 per year. The place was almost double in size to the previous Club home. In addition to a dozen bedrooms, there was more space for a library, a larger dining room, a theater, a billiard room with space for eight tables, and even a bowling alley.

Although the Club flourished in its new setting, all was not well on the financial front. The restaurant operated at a loss for several years. By 1891, the condition was serious enough for a group of members to prepare a detailed circular and send it anonymously to the full membership, at their own expense. In response, the Council appointed a committee of seven to investigate. The committee produced two copious reports, one from the majority and one from the minority. One principal difference between the two reports was the recommendation that the Club hire a professional manager to oversee day-to-day operations. At the 1891 annual meeting, several new Council members were elected from the "opposition slate." In June of that year, James W. Alexander was elected president of the Club and David L. Haight chairman of the House Committee.

Warships in the Hudson River for the dedication of the General Grant National Memorial, 1897

At the annual meeting in 1892, a proposal to increase the dues (to $75 for resident members) was defeated. (Not until 1972 did the Council gain the authority to change the dues structure without a vote of the membership.) In the fall of 1892, Edward Gleason was hired as the first superintendent (general manager) of the Club. With new leadership in place, the financial picture improved.

In 1897, when the General Grant National Memorial on Riverside Drive was to be dedicated, the courtesies of the Club were extended to the officers of the U.S. Army and Navy, as well as the foreign naval officers coming to the city for the festivities. An invitation was also extended to the whole Grant family, the president, vice-president, Supreme Court justices and the governor. How many of these worthies actually made use of the Club is unclear, although one group of officers from the USS *Texas* did so.

With the Club continuing to attract new members, the constitutional limit on membership was increased in

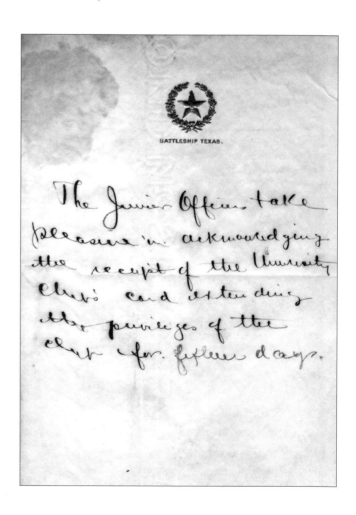

St. Luke's Hospital, which once stood on the land at Fifth Avenue and 54th Street now occupied by the clubhouse

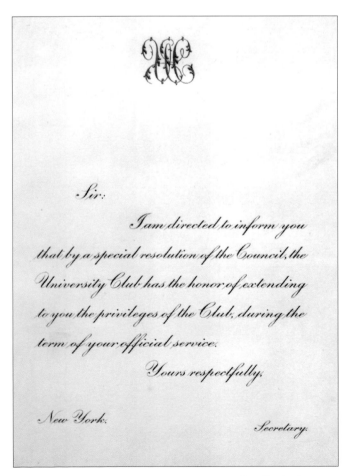

Form letter, with a script logo, used to advise public officials that they were welcome at the Club

1886, 1887, 1890, and 1892. By 1896, the Club was full, with 1,200 resident and 900 non-resident members, and there were 560 men on the waiting list. A new, larger clubhouse was clearly needed and there was a desire for a place with room for athletic facilities (other than bowling).

After considering a number of alternatives, in May 1896 the Council determined to purchase five lots, each measuring 125 x 100 feet, at the northwest corner of 54th Street and Fifth Avenue from St. Luke's Hospital, which had moved uptown. The total purchase price was $675,000. A detailed letter was sent to the membership describing the amenities to be included in the new building and explaining the reason for the move. The letter included an assurance that the cost of constructing and operating the new facility could be supported without any increase in the dues, but assumed that several hundred new members would be admitted. In 1897, the limit on resident members was increased to 1,700 and non-resident to 1,300 in anticipation of the move.

UNIVERSITY CLUB

SATURDAY, MARCH 19, 1892.

HOT

Chicken Consommé en tasse
Petit Bouchés de Terrapin, Newburg
Croquettes de Volaille
Oysters à la poulette

COLD

Kennebec Salmon à la Renaissance
Galantines de Capon en bellevue
Chaud froid de foie-gras à la Chevet
Filet of Beef larded à la jardinière
Ribs of Beef
Breast of Turkey au cresson
Tongue and Ham à la gelée
Salade of Lobster
Chicken Mayonnaise
Assorted Sandwiches

SWEET DISHES

Bisque Tortoni, Fancy Cakes, Fruits
Demi-tasse

UNIVERSITY CLUB CHAMPAGNE PUNCH
CLARET PUNCH

Menu with an early Club logo

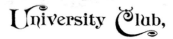

University Club,

MADISON AVENUE & 26TH STREET.

———

NEW YORK, February 10, 1893.

DEAR SIR :

The House Committee has arranged for a "Smoking Concert," in the Club House, on Saturday evening, February 18, 1893.

MUSIC BY THE NEW YORK PHILHARMONIC CLUB.

The Concert will begin promptly at 8.30 P. M.; Cakes and Ale will be served at 10.30 P. M.

Yours very truly,

HUGH D. AUCHINCLOSS,
SECRETARY.

Programme.

❀

PART FIRST.

1. SEXTETTE,   "SOMMERFAHRT,"   H. ZOELLNER
     1. Waldesruhe,
     2. Muhlengesang.
     3. Bauerntanz.

NEW YORK PHILHARMONIC CLUB.

2. VIOLONCELLO SOLO, (a) Nocturne op. 9, No. 2.   CHOPIN
     (b) Papillon,   D. POPPER

MR. PAUL MIERSCH.

3. (a) Patronille enfantine.   E. GILLET
   (b) Bilder aus dem Süden.   L. NICOLE

NEW YORK PHILHARMONIC CLUB.

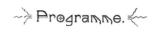

Programme.

❀

PART SECOND.

1. QUARTETTE.   "VARIATIONS," OP. 18, No. 5,   BEETHOVEN

TWO VIOLINS. VIOLA AND VIOLONCELLO.

2. FLUTE SOLO, (a) Largo,   HANDEL
     (b) Allegro,   DEMVEBEMANN

MR. EUGENE WEINER.

3. LIEBESTRAUM   A. CZIBULKA

4. SLAVONIC DANCE No. 8,   A. DVORJAK

NEW YORK PHILHARMONIC CLUB.

Invitation and program for the first concert hosted by the Club

*Letter from Club secretary Woolsey Johnson advising Mr. Brownell that he
has been elected a member of the Committee on Admissions*

UNIVERSITY CLUB

Carte du Jour

SATURDAY, JULY 18, 1891.

Little Neck Clams 10

SOUPS

Cup Cold Consommé in jelly or liquid 15   Cup Clam Broth à la Béchamel 15
Consommé à la d'Orsay 20—35   Croûte au pot 25—45
Cream of Green Corn 25—45

RELISHES

Pâté de foie-gras 50—1 00   New Tomatoes 25
Sardines 25   Radishes 10   Anchovies 20   Chutney 10   Olives 15
Stuffed Mangoes 15   Canapé de Caviar 25   Pickled Walnuts 10

FISH

Cold Salmon, tartar sauce 30—50
Soft Shell Crabs (each) 15
Filet of Sole fried à la Horly 25—45
Escalope of Sea Bass au vin blanc 25—45
Boiled Red Snapper, lobster sauce 25—45

RELEVÉ

Boiled Fowl with salt pork 45—85

ENTRÉES

Filet mignon à la Provençale 55—1 00
Escalope of Veal à la Milanaise 40—75
Salmis of Golden Plover with olives (each) 45
Spring Lamb Stew, Irish style 40—75

ROAST

Ribs of Beef 30—50   Stuffed Duckling, apple sauce 75—1 40

GAME AND POULTRY

Roast Chicken 1 30   Duckling 75—1 40   Spring Broilers 60-1 10
Golden Plover 40   Large Yellow-leg Snipe 60
Squab 60
(All Birds will be Roasted unless otherwise Ordered.)

COLD DISHES

Lobster, plain 30—50
Ribs of Beef 30—50   Corned Beef 20—35   Boned Chicken 40—75
Chicken 60—1 00   Ham 20—35   Tongue 20—35   Turkey 30—50
Corned Beef Tongue 20—35   Sirloin of Beef 30-50   Lamb, mint sauce 35—65

SALADS

Chicory 20   Romaine 25
Watercress 15   Potato 15   Cucumber 25   Lettuce 20
Chicken 40—75   Lobster 35—60
MAYONNAISE 10 CENTS EXTRA

CAFÉ NOIR 10 CENTS

VEGETABLES

New Green Corn 25   Stewed Corn 25
New Egg Plant 20   Cauliflower 30
Spinach Omelette 25   Green Peas 25
Cêpes à la Bordelaise 40   String Beans 25   Tomatoes stewed 20
Macaroni à l'Italienne 20 au gratin 20   Corn Fritters 15
Mashed Yellow Turnips 20   Fried Hominy 10   Spinach 25
Squash 20   Artichokes, (each) 40
Boiled Rice 10   Boiled Onions 10   Beets 10
Boiled New Potatoes 10   Potatoes sauté 15   Baked Potatoes split and sauté 15
POTATOES: à la Lyonaise 15   fried 10   Parisienne 15
Mashed 10   Mashed brown, stewed, Duchesse, hashed and baked 15
Potato Croquettes, each 10   Saratoga Potatoes 10

FRUITS AND DESSERT

Muskmelon, half 45   quarter 25   Peaches and cream 30   Blackberries 25
Raspberries 20   Watermelon 20   Cherries 20
Lalla Rookh 25
Stewed Prunes 20   Ice Cream and Cake 25
Pickled Pears, (2) 20   Oranges 10
Omelette Soufflée 50   aux confitures 35   au rhum 35

CHEESE

Neufchâtel 10   Gruyère 10   Camembert 15   Roquefort 15
American 10   Brie 10   Gorgonzola 20

DISHES TO ORDER

Small Sirloin Steak	40	English Mutton Chop, each	30
Sirloin steak, plain	60	Mutton chops breaded, tomato s'ce, each	25
Sirloin steak with tomato sauce	70	Mutton chops à la jardinière "	25
Sirloin steak with piquante sauce	70	Mutton chops with peas "	25
Sirloin steak with olives	85	Mutton chops à la soubise "	30
Sirloin steak with mushrooms	90	Calf's Brains au beurre noir	30—50
Sirloin steak with cêpes	90	Calf's head à la vinaigrette	40
Extra Sirloin steak	1 20	Calf's head à la poulette	60
University Club Sirloin Steak	1 80	Calf's head, piquante sauce	50
Porterhouse steak	1 25	Calf's head, tomato sauce	60
Extra Porterhouse steak	2 25	Sweetbreads, broiled	50
Filet of beef, plain	75	Sweetbreads à la jardinière	60
Filet of beef with tomato sauce	85	Sweetbreads breaded, tomato sauce	60
Filet of beef à la Béarnaise	1 00	Sweetbreads with mushrooms	80
Filet of beef à la Bordelaise	1 00	Sweetbreads with truffles	1 50
Filet of beef with cêpes	1 00	Chicken sauté, chasseur	90—1 75
Filet of beef with mushrooms	1 00	Chicken sauté à l'Espagnole	90—1 75
Filet of beef with truffles	1 50	Chicken sauté à la Marengo	90—1 75
Filet Châteaubriand	1 50	Chicken fricassée, mushrooms	90—1 75
Lamb chops, each	15	Chicken fricassée with rice	90—1 75
Spring Lamb Chops, each	20	Chicken croquettes, each	25
Mutton chops plain, each	15		

Omelette, plain 20   aux fines herbes 25   with ham or cheese 30

Omelette, Spanish style, with kidneys, with peas or Chicken livers 40

À la carte menu, 1891

Jun 11/95

UNIVERSITY CLUB

WINE LIST.

Rhine.

	Qts.	Pts.
11—Steinberger Cabinet, Goldbecher Auslese, Manskopf Sarasin	6 15	
2—Johannisberger Cabinet, yellow seal,...D. Leiden	2 40	
4—Rauenthaler Berg Auslese, ... Manskopf Sarasin	2 35	1 25
19—Marcobrunner, Grafen von Shoenborn, ... Manskopf Sarasin	2 25	1 15
20—Marcobrunner,............. ....D. Leiden	2 10	
22—Steinwein, in Bocksbeutel,.................D. Leiden........	1 90	1 00
5—Schloss Vollradser,....................Manskopf Sarasin	1 70	95
17—Liebfraumilch ....D. Leiden	1 70	95
21—Steinwein, in Bocksbeutel, ...Manskopf Sarasin	1 35	70
9—Hochheimer .... .D. Leiden........	1 15	65
18—Niersteiner.............................D. Leiden........	1 00	55
3—Laubenheimer.......... ....D. Leiden	95	55

Moselle.

6—Piesporter.......... ....D. Leiden........	80	45
10—Brauneberger ....D. Leiden.......·	75	45
12—Sparkling Moselle Muscatelle........D. Leiden	2 30	1 25

Sherry.

100—Old Oloroso, bottled 1850, Starin Sherry	4 00	
131—Old East India, bottled 1856, Starin Sherry.................	4 00	
99—Old Amontillado, Solera Palma..........................	1 40	75
101—Bininger...	75	40

Bordeaux—White.

1. 49 16—Haut Sauternes, 1874,............... ....Clossman & Co...	1 40	75 *3- ·2*
6. 58 25—Sauternes, Premières....................Clossman & Co...	80	45 *5 ·* *7*
24 - 33 58—Sauternes,....................... ....University Club..	50	30 *5- 2/6*
17. 20 1—Graves, ...University Club..	50	30 *13*

WINES AND LIQUORS BY THE CASE AT REDUCED PRICES

Late 19th-century wine list, with an impressive assortment of wines

stock

qts. pts.

Bordeaux—Red.

		Qts.	Pts.
63—Château Margaux, 1870,	Du Vivier & Co...	4 80	
37— " Mouton, 1870,	Du Vivier & Co...	4 40	
41— " Lafite, 1875,	Eyber & De Sarrau	5 50	
29— " Mouton Rothschild, 1880,	J. Calvet & Co...	4 20	
60— " Latour, 1878,	W. H. Fearing..	3 75	
32—St Emilion,	Arnaud Petrus...	3 15	
14—Château Mouton Rothschild, 1878,	A. de Luze & Fils.	3 60	
43— " Lafite, 1878, Alex.	Andreae, Kraay & Co	2 75	
28— " Margaux, 1877,	J. Calvet & Co ...	2 50	1 30
30— " Haut Brion, 1890,	W. H. Fearing..	2 40	
23—Pichon Longueville, 1870,	Clossman & Co ...		1 15
65—Château Lagrange, 1880,	J. Calvet & Co	1 90	
31— " Rauzan, 1890	V. M. Eyber....	1 75	95
34— " Pichon Longueville, 1890	V. M. Eyber....	1 40	75
15—Château Beychevelle, 1881,	University Club..	1 05	60
59— " Lagrange, 1881,	University Club..	1 05	60
60—Pontet-Canet, 1881,	University Club..	90	50
13—Château de Pez, 1887,	Barton & Guestier.	95	55
8— " Malleret, 1881,	Clossman & Co..	90	50
27—St. Julien, 1881,	Barton & Guestier.	80	45
36—St Estèphe,	Clossman & Co ..	75	45
61—Margaux,	Charles H. Arnold.	65	40
57—Première,	University Club..	60	30
62—Ordinaire, St. Emilion,	Cunliffe, Dobson & Co	45	25

Champagne.

26—UNIVERSITY CLUB, Very Dry, Vintage 1889		2 55	1 40
per case, Quarts $28 20—Pints $ 30 20			
51—Pommery & Greno, Nature		3 70	1 95
80— " Sec		3 40	1 80
68—Moët & Chandon, Dry Imperial, Cuvée 36,		3 55	
72— " " Brut Imperial		3 45	1 85
71— " " White Seal		3 05	1 65
84—Ruinart, Vin Brut	Half pints 95.	3 30	1 75
81— " Maréchale		3 00	1 65
74—L. Roederer, Grand Vin Sec		3 40	1 80
75— " Brut		3 40	1 80
82—Giesler, Brut		3 40	1 80
83— " Extra Superior, Very Dry		3 15	1 70
85— " Green Label			1 65
91—G. H. Mumm, Extra Dry,		3 20	1 70
78—Irroy, Vin Brut		3 30	1 75
77— " Grand Extra Dry		3 15	1 70
98—Gold Lack, Sec		3 10	1 70
97— " Brut		3 00	1 70
89—Perrier-Jouët, Extra Dry Special	Half Pints 90	3 20	1 70
87— " Reserve Dry	Magnums, 5 95	3 20	1 70
88— " Vin Brut		3 20	1 70
92—Delbeck & Co., Brut		3 25	1 75
96—St. Marceaux, Brut		3 15	
94—Royal Charter			1 70
73—Binet Sec		2 95	
110—Special, Extra Dry, H. B. K		1 25	70

Burgundy—White.

44—Chablis	F. Chauvenet	1 15	65

Burgundy—Red.

124—Clos de Vougeot, 1865,	F. Chauvenet ...	4 50	
125—Chambertin, 1865,	F. Chauvenet ...	3 35	
55—Clos de Vougeot, 1874,	F. Chauvenet ...	2 90	
56—Chambertin, 1874,	F. Chauvenet ...	2 85	1 50
66—Chambertin, 1885,	F. Chauvenet ...	2 00	1 05
67—Chambertin, 1881,	F. Chauvenet ...		1 00
39—Hermitage, 1878,	C. Marey & Co ...	1 60	85

WINES AND LIQUORS BY THE CASE AT REDUCED PRICES

---

sold

stock

qts. pts.

Burgundy—Red, Continued.

		Qts.	Pts.
45—Beaune, 1885,	F Chauvenet...	1 20	60
46—Pommard, 1878,	University Club..	1 00	55
40—Macon,	University Club..	75	40

Port.

52—B. O. Fino		1 35	

Madeira.

103—Southside		1 80	95
48—Castle B.		1 70	

Hungarian—White.

70—Somlyai, 1885,	Hossfeld & Wierl.	70	

Hungarian—Red.

93—Budai, Sup., 1880,	Hossfeld & Wierl.	1 00	
79—Szegszárdi, 1886,	Hossfeld & Wierl.	60	35
95—Budai Vörös,		60	35

Austrian—Red.

53—Vöslauer Goldeck, Cabinet	R. Schlumberger..	1 55	
54—Vöslauer Goldeck,	R. Schlumberger..	1 25	

California.

76—Eclipse, (Sparkling)		1 50	90
33—Cabinet Riesling, (White)		60	35
55—Las Palmas, 1889,		60	35
24—Zinfandel, (Red)		55	30

Brandy.

104—Savillac, 1803,		4 90	
105— " 1825		3 50	
106—S. O. P.		2 50	
107—Maret		2 00	
123—Blackberry		1 25	
121—Apple		1 00	

Whiskey.

111—Antediluvian Rye		2 10	
108—Old Reserve Rye, 1860, (Imp. quarts)	Edw. B. Bruce & Co.,	2 00	
64—Old Stock Rye.		1 80	
109—Hannisville Unblended Rye		1 25	
86—Somerset Club Rye		1 10	
112—"Pepper" Bourbon		1 25	
127—King William IV., V O. P. Scotch		2 10	
113—Vice Regal Blend Scotch.		1 40	
115—Glenlivet Scotch, Special Reserve		1 40	
128—Sir John Power & Son, Ⓟ Dublin Whiskey ...		1 40	
114—Irish		1 25	

Rum.

118—Antigua, 1847		3 75	
116—Old Grenada, 1847		3 75	
119—Jamaica		1 25	
120—St Croix		1 25	
122—Medford.		1 00	

Gin.

117—A. V. H		1 90	
129—Plymouth		1 25	
130—Old Tom Gin		1 00	

WINES AND LIQUORS BY THE CASE AT REDUCED PRICES

Late 19th-century wine list, inside spread

III

McKIM'S ITALIAN PALACE

by Percy Preston Jr.

Taken from 42nd Street, this early 20th century view of the clubhouse (behind St. Thomas Church) shows the original roof garden.

In designing a new clubhouse for The University Club, Charles McKim of the firm McKim, Mead & White was influenced by the architecture of the Italian Renaissance, which he knew well from his visits to Italy. Although the typical palazzo of the era would have had three floors, the requirements of the Club mandated a much taller building. McKim's genius was to divide the façade of the new building into three parts separated by stringcourses. Each part has a major floor with large windows, and lesser floors with small windows. Thus, a nine-story building was enclosed in a skin that paid homage to the Renaissance.

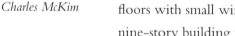

Charles McKim

The scholar Leland Roth wrote of The University Club, "the basic motifs come from Renaissance Italy, but the reference here is not as much to the Italy of the visual arts as the place where humanistic learning and discourse were revived. Elements from the Palazzo Spannochi, Siena, and the Palazzo Albergati, Bologna, are freely quoted." The architectural historian Mosette Broderick wrote, "in the end, McKim…created a sort of Palazzo Strozzi [Florence] with a soupçon of five other palaces on the outside." She also wrote, "The University Club remains as one of New York City's best buildings."

The building is constructed of pink Milford granite, the same type of stone used in the Boston Public Library, an earlier McKim, Mead & White

commission. The clubhouse would wind up costing $2,043,756 (approximately $50,000,000 today). This was funded, in large part, by a loan from the Equitable Life Assurance Society secured by a mortgage on the property.

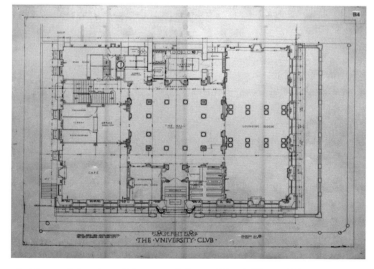

Architectural drawing of the ground floor of the clubhouse. The two rows of columns in the Reading Room (right) were not built.

Above: Main Atrium, ca. 1900
Right: Detail of Atrium today

Above: Main Dining Room, 1914
Right: Main Dining Room today

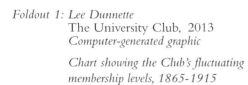

Foldout 1: Lee Dunnette
      The University Club, 2013
      Computer-generated graphic

      Chart showing the Club's fluctuating
      membership levels, 1865-1915

Foldout 2: Main Room of the Library, with its murals
      and decorative panels by H. Siddons Mawbray

      The central dome of the Library

Top: Reading Room, ca. 1900
Bottom: Percy S. Douglas Members Reading Room today

Top: Tap Room, 1933
Bottom left: What is now the Tap Room was once used for billiards. Bottom right: The current Billiards Room adjacent to the Tap Room

Top: Chess/Conversation Room today
Right: The same space, mid-20th century

Top: Council Room, ca. 1912
Bottom: Backgammon room on the ground floor in the 1930s. Today, this is the Dwight Lounge.

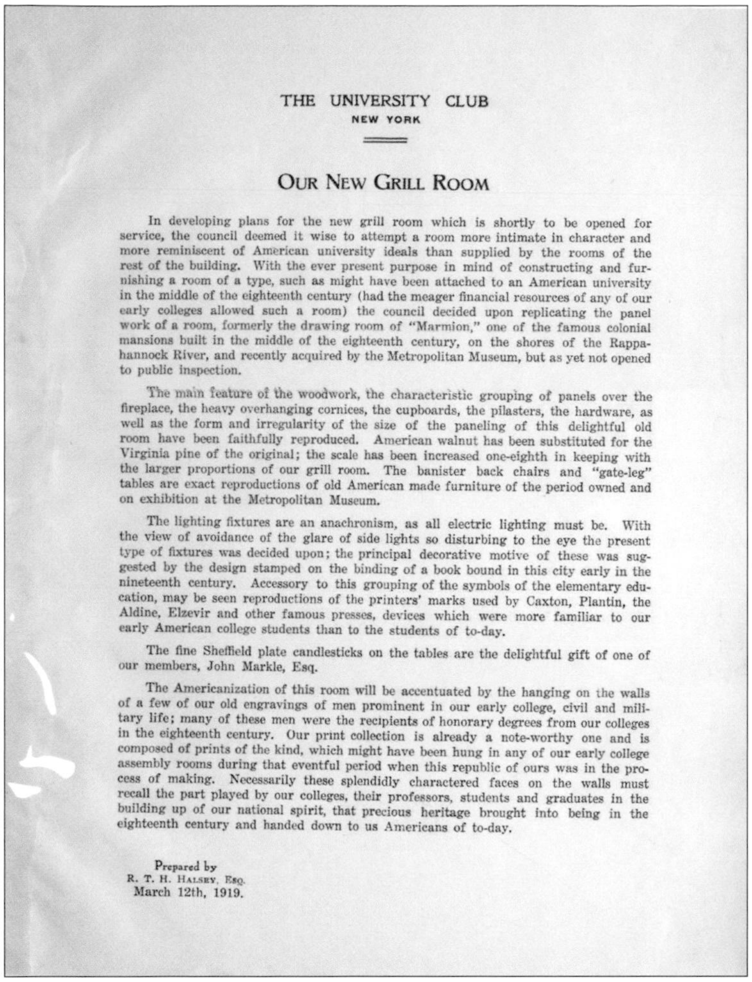

THE UNIVERSITY CLUB
NEW YORK

Our New Grill Room

In developing plans for the new grill room which is shortly to be opened for service, the council deemed it wise to attempt a room more intimate in character and more reminiscent of American university ideals than supplied by the rooms of the rest of the building. With the ever present purpose in mind of constructing and furnishing a room of a type, such as might have been attached to an American university in the middle of the eighteenth century (had the meager financial resources of any of our early colleges allowed such a room) the council decided upon replicating the panel work of a room, formerly the drawing room of "Marmion," one of the famous colonial mansions built in the middle of the eighteenth century, on the shores of the Rappahannock River, and recently acquired by the Metropolitan Museum, but as yet not opened to public inspection.

The main feature of the woodwork, the characteristic grouping of panels over the fireplace, the heavy overhanging cornices, the cupboards, the pilasters, the hardware, as well as the form and irregularity of the size of the paneling of this delightful old room have been faithfully reproduced. American walnut has been substituted for the Virginia pine of the original; the scale has been increased one-eighth in keeping with the larger proportions of our grill room. The banister back chairs and "gate-leg" tables are exact reproductions of old American made furniture of the period owned and on exhibition at the Metropolitan Museum.

The lighting fixtures are an anachronism, as all electric lighting must be. With the view of avoidance of the glare of side lights so disturbing to the eye the present type of fixtures was decided upon; the principal decorative motive of these was suggested by the design stamped on the binding of a book bound in this city early in the nineteenth century. Accessory to this grouping of the symbols of the elementary education, may be seen reproductions of the printers' marks used by Caxton, Plantin, the Aldine, Elzevir and other famous presses, devices which were more familiar to our early American college students than to the students of to-day.

The fine Sheffield plate candlesticks on the tables are the delightful gift of one of our members, John Markle, Esq.

The Americanization of this room will be accentuated by the hanging on the walls of a few of our old engravings of men prominent in our early college, civil and military life; many of these men were the recipients of honorary degrees from our colleges in the eighteenth century. Our print collection is already a note-worthy one and is composed of prints of the kind, which might have been hung in any of our early college assembly rooms during that eventful period when this republic of ours was in the process of making. Necessarily these splendidly charactered faces on the walls must recall the part played by our colleges, their professors, students and graduates in the building up of our national spirit, that precious heritage brought into being in the eighteenth century and handed down to us Americans of to-day.

Prepared by
R. T. H. Halsey, Esq.
March 12th, 1919.

Top: Dwight Dining Room today
Bottom: This room when it was the Grill

One elegant work of art both decorative and commemorative, apt to be overlooked because of its small size (and now hung in the Library elevator vestibule), is the Building Committee roundels. This piece, which James Alexander rightfully thought suitable for illustrating in his first history of the Club, recognizes the work of the Building Committee in charge of the erection of the 54th Street clubhouse. It can be said that the work successfully combines American sculpture and wood furniture elements. The two cast bronze roundels were made by the Gorham foundry and have their stamp. The left one recites the names of the Building Committee and their years spanned in that endeavor as 1896–1900, within a wreath-like surround cast with running husks and berries interspersed with rosettes. The right medallion is cast with the Club's seal of two youths grasping hands in friendship before a classical statue of Athena, a banderole with the club motto "In Fellowship Lies Friendship" in Greek above. The two roundels are set within a surround of the same beautifully figured old-growth oak as adorns many of The University Club's rooms, all within a frame crisply carved to match the bronze—an elegant little American beaux arts object indeed, in every way evocative of the designs of its time.

—Timothy Hamilton

College Hall, 2014

The clubhouse early in the 20th century. In 1910, the balustrade was removed at the insistence of the city, to widen the sidewalk.

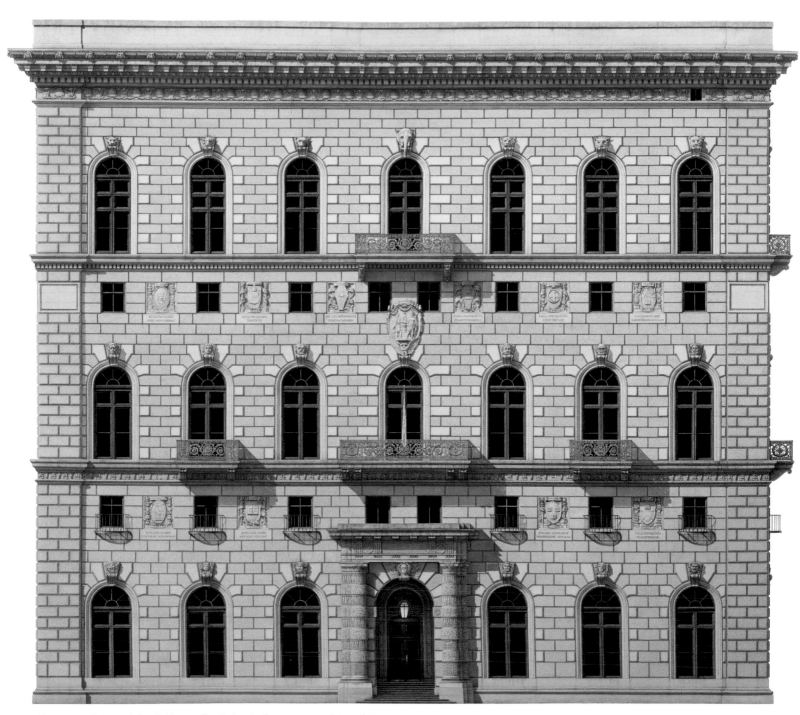

Above: Rendering of the clubhouse façade by Andrew Zega and Bernd Dams, 2011

IV

CLUB LIFE

by Percy Preston Jr.

Above: This illustration by Norman Rockwell appeared on the cover of *The Saturday Evening Post* on August 27, 1960. **Left:** The clubhouse decorated for a parade honoring Admiral George Dewey, hero of the Spanish-American War, and a member of The University Club

From original menus, we can see how members dined. Invitations tell us who came to speak, or to be honored. Programs shed light on concerts and loan exhibits of artworks. Announcements tell of new facilities or changes in practices. Press clippings report on new initiatives, such as the first-ever dinner dance. The Club's archive blesses us with an abundance of material to help paint the picture of how our forefathers lived.

Prince Henry of Prussia

1902

Dinner in honour of
His Royal Highness
Prince Henry of Prussia
by
The University Club
of the City of New York
March the seventh
1902

MENU

Little Neck clams

Bisque de crabes à la Norfolk
Consommé à la Washington

Céleri   Amandes salées   Olives pimentos

Planked shad, maître d'hôtel

Noisettes d'agneau à la Meteor
Petits pois   Pommes de terre de la Bermude

Champignons à l'Université

Sorbet à l'Impériale

Suprême de vo.   la Toulouse
Asperges froi   e

Fromage

Glace en surprise   Fruit

Café

Photograph after a portrait, now lost, by an unknown artist.
Inscribed: "The University Club New York in remembrance of my visit to the
club March 7, 1902" and signed by the prince.

The prince was on a goodwill visit to the United States, and while in New
York, oversaw the launching of a racing yacht commissioned by his brother,
Kaiser Wilhelm II. The leadership of the Club hosted a banquet in the
prince's honor. Ninety people attended, with Club members being charged
$30 each (at a time when annual dues were $60). At a reception later in the
evening open to all members, a thousand men showed up, according to
James Alexander's history of the Club.

The Arctic Explorer

1904

UNIVERSITY CLUB.

CLUB NIGHT.

SATURDAY EVENING, MARCH 5TH, 1904,
AT NINE O'CLOCK.

COMMANDER ROBERT E. PEARY
WILL DELIVER AN ADDRESS ON THE SUBJECT OF
ARCTIC EXPLORATION,
ILLUSTRATED WITH COLORED VIEWS.

SUPPER WILL BE SERVED.

Robert Peary was the first man to reach the North Pole,
doing so in April 1909, after several unsuccessful attempts.

The Officers and the Governor

1906

New York governor Frank W. Higgins was entertained by his
military staff at the Club in 1906.

The Club in World War I

1917

In April 1917, after the United States entered into World War I, The University Club made an effort to record its members' participation in the war effort, both in and out of uniform. Members were invited to submit information about their branch of service, rank, or details of their war-related work in the civilian sector. The Library staff transferred the information to handwritten cards, one for each Club member. In time, the collection grew to several hundred entries and took up two drawers in the Library's card catalogue.

The largest number of uniformed men was from the army, with a smaller number in the navy. Their military ranks range from private up to major general. There were also small groups of men who served overseas with the Red Cross and the Y.M.C.A. The cards also include other bits of information, such as a piece of onion skin paper behind the card for "Davis, Chandler H'88, captain, U. S. Army Engineers," recording that he was awarded the British Military Cross for heroism. Whether he was also awarded an American decoration is not noted.

Unfortunately, not all of the information is celebratory. Twenty members of the Club were killed in action. Their names are honored in the Main Atrium of the clubhouse.

One card of note in the military drawer reads "Wilson, Woodrow P'79, President of the United States, Commander in Chief of the Army & Navy of the United States." Wilson joined the Club in 1903, when he was president of Princeton University, and remained a member until his death in 1924.

If Wilson had not already been a member of the Club, once he was elected president of the United States he would have been named an honorary member, as it was Club policy at the time to offer such memberships to the president, vice president, justices of the U.S. Supreme Court and certain military and naval officers during their respective terms of office.

Club members also served in a variety of civilian war-related occupations. Some served on draft boards, and others were alien property custodians. Members were with the diplomatic service in Paris, and worked for the U.S. Food Administration and the U.S. Fuel Administration. One member was the assistant secretary of the treasury and another was the U.S. ambassador in London.

One card of note in the military drawer reads "Wilson, Woodrow P'79, President of the United States, Commander in Chief of the Army & Navy of the United States."

The Club made a gift to the American Field Service in France to cover the cost of ambulance #622, as attested by an elegant certificate (facing page).

For the duration of the war, the Council voted to remit payment of dues for all members on active service, resulting in a drop of $22,400 in dues income for the year 1918. To put this in perspective, annual dues were then $100 for resident members, $50 for non-residents, and $35 for army and navy members. Total dues for the year were $245,410, so this accommodation resulted in a decline in dues income of almost 10 percent.

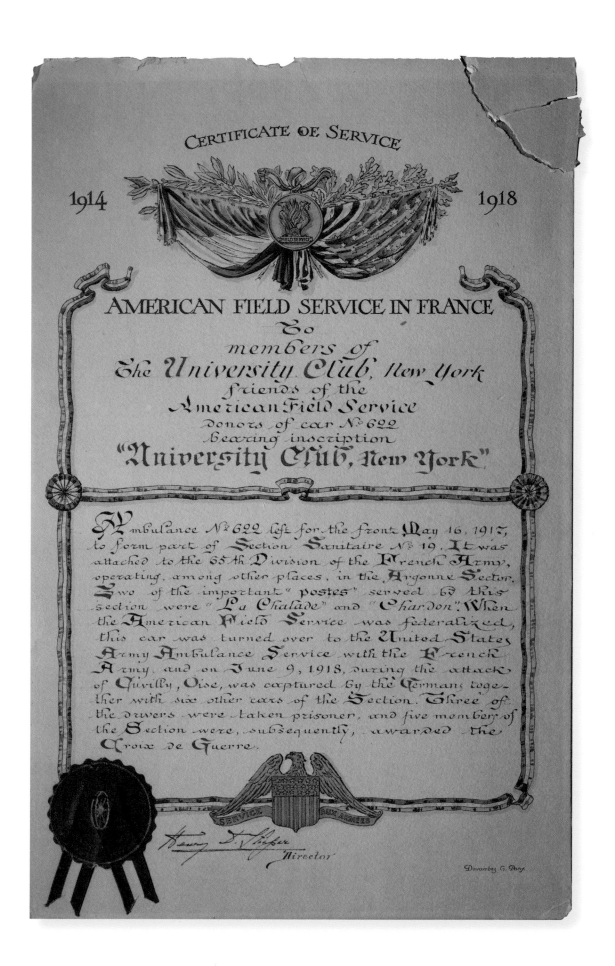

CERTIFICATE OF SERVICE

1914 1918

AMERICAN FIELD SERVICE IN FRANCE
To
members of
The University Club, New York
friends of the
American Field Service
donors of car N° 622
bearing inscription
"University Club, New York"

Ambulance N° 622 left for the front May 16, 1917, to form part of Section Sanitaire N° 19. It was attached to the 65th Division of the French Army, operating, among other places, in the Argonne Sector. Two of the important "postes" served by this section were "La Chalade" and "Chardon". When the American Field Service was federalized, this car was turned over to the United States Army Ambulance Service with the French Army, and on June 9, 1918, during the attack of Ouvilly, Oise, was captured by the Germans together with six other cars of the Section. Three of the drivers were taken prisoner, and five members of the Section were, subsequently, awarded the Croix de Guerre.

SERVICE AUX ARMÉES

Henry D. Sleeper
Director

Devambez G. Paris.

General Pershing's Letter

1919

AMERICAN EXPEDITIONARY FORCES
OFFICE OF THE COMMANDER-IN-CHIEF

New York, September 11, 1919.

Mr. H. Hobart Porter, Vice Pres.,
        The University Club,
            New York City.

My dear Mr. Porter:

    I desire to thank the Council

of the University Club for their

action in according me the privileges

of honorary membership, and to express

my deep appreciation of this courtesy.

        Very sincerely yours,

        John J. Pershing

General of the Armies John J. Pershing commanded all U.S. forces in
Europe during World War I.

The Admiral

1920

THE UNIVERSITY CLUB

FIFTH AVENUE AND 54TH STREET
NEW YORK

RECEPTION TO ADMIRAL JELLICOE

ON SATURDAY EVENING, JANUARY 3RD. 1920
AT 9:30 O'CLOCK
ADMIRAL OF THE FLEET
VISCOUNT JELLICOE, OF SCAPA.
G. C. B., O. M., G. C. V. O.,
WHO COMMANDED THE BRITISH FLEET IN THE BATTLE OF JUTLAND
WILL BE THE GUEST OF THE UNIVERSITY CLUB
AT A RECEPTION IN HIS HONOR

30 DECEMBER, 1919   THE ENTERTAINMENT COMMITTEE

Franklin D. Roosevelt served as Assistant Secretary of the Navy
from 1913 to 1920, and in that capacity attended the dinner honoring
Admiral Jellicoe.

Visitor's Letter

1919

H.M.S. Renown

New York.

21st November 1919.

Rear Admiral Sir Lionel Halsey begs
to thank the House Committee of the
University Club **for** their kindness
in extending to him the privileges
of the Club House for the period of
seven days.

When the Prince of Wales (later Duke of Windsor) paid a visit to New York City in 1919, the battle cruiser HMS *Renown* anchored in the Hudson River to serve as his quarters. Although the prince did not visit the Club, the Club extended an offer of hospitality to the officers of the *Renown* and of the ships accompanying her. This is one of the acknowledgment letters received.

Wickersham & Taft

1922

Luncheon to
The Rt. Hon. Senator G. F. Pearce, P. C. of Australia
Minister for home and territory and the Australian
delegate to the Conference for limitation of armament
and
Hon. George W. Wickersham
February 11, 1922

G. F. Pearce
Guy Innes
Henry W. Nevinson

Luncheon to
William H. Taft
Chief Justice of the United States
February 18, 1922

George W. Wickersham served as Attorney General of the United States in the Taft administration, and was president of The University Club from 1928 to 1930.

William Howard Taft was President of the United States from 1909 to 1913, and Chief Justice of the United States from 1921 to 1930.

Menus

1923 – 1930

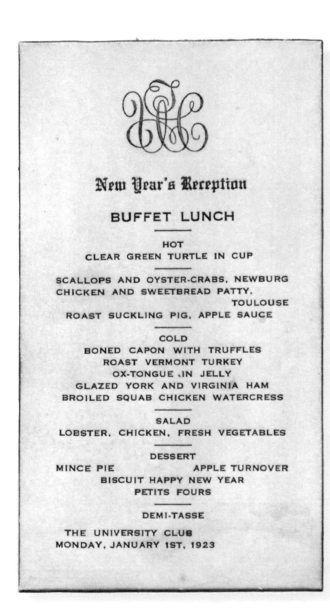

New Year's Reception

BUFFET LUNCH

HOT
CLEAR GREEN TURTLE IN CUP

SCALLOPS AND OYSTER-CRABS, NEWBURG
CHICKEN AND SWEETBREAD PATTY,
TOULOUSE
ROAST SUCKLING PIG, APPLE SAUCE

COLD
BONED CAPON WITH TRUFFLES
ROAST VERMONT TURKEY
OX-TONGUE ,IN JELLY
GLAZED YORK AND VIRGINIA HAM
BROILED SQUAB CHICKEN WATERCRESS

SALAD
LOBSTER, CHICKEN, FRESH VEGETABLES

DESSERT
MINCE PIE   APPLE TURNOVER
BISCUIT HAPPY NEW YEAR
PETITS FOURS

DEMI-TASSE

THE UNIVERSITY CLUB
MONDAY, JANUARY 1ST, 1923

CLUB NIGHT

MENU

HOT
CLEAR GREEN TURTLE AU XERES

LOBSTER AND OYSTER CRABS, NEWBURG

COLD
FOIE GRAS DE STRASBOURG
YORK AND VIRGINIA HAM IN JELLY
SUPREME OF YOUNG GUINEA, MONTMORENCY
ROAST VERMONT TURKEY AU CRESSON
PATE OF GAME, ST. HUBERT
BONED TRUFFLED CAPON
OX-TONGUE UNIVERSITY

SALADS
SHRIMP   CHICKEN   VEGETABLE   FRUIT

STRAWBERRY SHORT CAKE
MACAROON BISCUIT GLACE
PETITS FOURS

DEMI-TASSE

TUESDAY, APRIL 15, 1930
THE UNIVERSITY GLEE CLUB

The logo on this lunch menu from 1923 includes a "T" as in "The University Club." By 1930, the logo used by the Club would be familiar to members today.

Lunch Speakers

Various Dates

THE UNIVERSITY CLUB
NEW YORK

———

DWIGHT W. MORROW

WHO HAS BEEN IN GOVERNMENT SERVICE IN ENGLAND AND FRANCE
DURING THE PAST YEAR

WILL BE OUR GUEST ON

SATURDAY, FEBRUARY 8, 1919

———

LUNCHEON AT $1.50 PER COVER WILL BE SERVED
PROMPTLY AT 1.30 P. M.   SPEAKING AT 2.15 P. M.
KINDLY INDICATE ON THE ENCLOSED CARD YOUR
PROBABLE INTENTION TO BE PRESENT.

THE UNIVERSITY CLUB
NEW YORK

———

HIS EXCELLENCY THE RIGHT HONORABLE

THE EARL OF READING, G. C. B,

LORD CHIEF JUSTICE OF ENGLAND

BRITISH AMBASSADOR EXTRAORDINARY AND PLENIPOTENTIARY

ON SPECIAL MISSION AND HIGH COMMISSIONER IN THE

UNITED STATES OF AMERICA.

WILL BE OUR GUEST AT LUNCHEON ON

SATURDAY, MARCH 29, 1919

For many decades, the Club hosted a succession of Saturday luncheon speakers. These invitations (and those on the next page) are only a small representation of the many public officials, academics, diplomats, business leaders and military figures who came to the Club. James R. Garfield (next page) was the son of President James A. Garfield, who was assassinated in 1881. Dwight Morrow is best remembered today as the father-in-law of the aviator Charles Lindbergh.

THE UNIVERSITY CLUB
FIFTH AVENUE AND FIFTY-FOURTH STREET
NEW YORK

SATURDAY, JANUARY 6, 1923
PROMPTLY AT ONE-THIRTY O'CLOCK

LUNCHEON

THE GUESTS OF THE CLUB WILL BE

PRESIDENT LIVINGSTON FARRAND
OF CORNELL UNIVERSITY

PRESIDENT FREDERICK C. FERRY
OF HAMILTON COLLEGE

PRESIDENT GEORGE B. CUTTEN
OF COLGATE UNIVERSITY

SPEAKING WILL COMMENCE AT TWO-FIFTEEN O'CLOCK

IF YOU WILL BE PRESENT, IT WILL GREATLY ASSIST THE COMMITTEE IF YOU WILL SIGN AND RETURN THE ENCLOSED CARD

THE ENTERTAINMENT COMMITTEE.

THE UNIVERSITY CLUB
FIFTH AVENUE AND FIFTY-FOURTH STREET
NEW YORK

LUNCHEON

SATURDAY, FEBRUARY 5, 1927
PROMPTLY AT ONE-THIRTY O'CLOCK

THE GUEST OF THE CLUB WILL BE
HON. JAMES R. GARFIELD
FORMER SECRETARY OF THE INTERIOR

WHO WILL SPEAK ON

MEXICO

SPEAKING WILL COMMENCE AT TWO-FIFTEEN O'CLOCK

IF YOU WILL BE PRESENT, PLEASE SIGN AND RETURN THE ENCLOSED CARD.

THE ENTERTAINMENT COMMITTEE

THE UNIVERSITY CLUB
FIFTH AVENUE AND FIFTY-FOURTH STREET
NEW YORK

LUNCHEON

SATURDAY, FEBRUARY 7, 1925
PROMPTLY AT ONE-THIRTY O'CLOCK

THE GUEST OF THE CLUB WILL BE
COUNT BYRON DE PROVAK
WHO WILL GIVE A LECTURE ILLUSTRATED BY MOVING PICTURES ON
EXCAVATIONS OF CARTHAGE
AND
A TRIP TO THE DEAD CITIES OF THE SAHARA

SPEAKING WILL COMMENCE AT TWO-FIFTEEN O'CLOCK

IF YOU WILL BE PRESENT, PLEASE SIGN AND RETURN THE ENCLOSED CARD.

THE ENTERTAINMENT COMMITTEE

THE UNIVERSITY CLUB
NEW YORK

LUNCHEON

SATURDAY, JANUARY 19, 1929
PROMPTLY AT ONE-THIRTY O'CLOCK

THE GUEST OF THE CLUB WILL BE
PRESIDENT A. LAWRENCE LOWELL
OF HARVARD UNIVERSITY
WHO WILL SPEAK ON
SOME RECENT DEVELOPMENTS IN UNIVERSITY ORGANIZATION

SPEAKING WILL COMMENCE AT TWO-FIFTEEN O'CLOCK

IF YOU WILL BE PRESENT, PLEASE SIGN AND RETURN THE ENCLOSED CARD.

THE ENTERTAINMENT COMMITTEE

THE UNIVERSITY CLUB
FIFTH AVENUE AND FIFTY-FOURTH STREET
NEW YORK

LUNCHEON

SATURDAY, MARCH 20, 1926
PROMPTLY AT ONE-THIRTY O'CLOCK

THE GUESTS OF THE CLUB WILL BE

DEAN RADCLIFFE HEERMANCE
DIRECTOR OF ADMISSION, PRINCETON UNIVERSITY
AND
PROFESSOR ROBERT N. CORWIN
CHAIRMAN, COMMITTEE ON ADMISSIONS, YALE UNIVERSITY
WHO WILL SPEAK ON
THE PROBLEM OF LIMITING ENROLLMENT IN OUR COLLEGES
AND UNIVERSITIES, AND ITS EFFECT ON ADMISSION

SPEAKING WILL COMMENCE AT TWO-FIFTEEN O'CLOCK

IF YOU WILL BE PRESENT, PLEASE SIGN AND RETURN THE ENCLOSED CARD.

THE ENTERTAINMENT COMMITTEE

THE UNIVERSITY CLUB
NEW YORK

LUNCHEON

SATURDAY, JANUARY 16, 1932
PROMPTLY AT ONE-THIRTY O'CLOCK

THE GUEST OF THE CLUB WILL BE
POLICE COMMISSIONER EDWARD P. MULROONEY
WHO WILL SPEAK ON
CRIME IN NEW YORK CITY TO-DAY

SPEAKING WILL COMMENCE AT TWO-FIFTEEN O'CLOCK

IF YOU WILL BE PRESENT, PLEASE SIGN AND RETURN THE ENCLOSED CARD.

THE ENTERTAINMENT COMMITTEE

THE UNIVERSITY CLUB
NEW YORK

———

LUNCHEON

———

SATURDAY, DECEMBER 20, 1930
PROMPTLY AT ONE-THIRTY O'CLOCK

———

THE GUEST OF THE CLUB WILL BE
MR. RICHARD WHITNEY
PRESIDENT OF THE NEW YORK STOCK EXCHANGE
WHO WILL SPEAK ON
THE MARKET FOR SECURITIES
PROVIDED BY THE NEW YORK STOCK EXCHANGE

———

SPEAKING WILL COMMENCE AT TWO-FIFTEEN O'CLOCK

———

IF YOU WILL BE PRESENT, PLEASE SIGN AND RETURN THE
ENCLOSED CARD.

THE ENTERTAINMENT COMMITTEE

THE UNIVERSITY CLUB
NEW YORK

———

CLUB LUNCHEON

———

SATURDAY, DECEMBER 10, 1938
PROMPTLY AT ONE-THIRTY O'CLOCK

———

THE GUEST OF THE CLUB WILL BE
OUR FELLOW MEMBER

HON. HERBERT C. HOOVER

———

MEMBERS WHO EXPECT TO ATTEND ARE REQUESTED
TO RETURN THE ENCLOSED CARD PROMPTLY.

———

GUESTS MAY BE INVITED.

Top: Richard Whitney spoke at the Club fifteen months after the famous stock market crash of 1929. In 1938, Whitney was convicted of embezzlement and confined to Sing Sing prison for a number of years.

Bottom: Herbert Hoover was a member of the Club from 1917 to 1964 and spoke here on a number of occasions. In 1938, eight hundred men turned out to hear him, and his speech was amplified to several rooms within the clubhouse.

The Depression and Prohibition

The Eighteenth Amendment to the U.S. Constitution outlawing "the manufacture, sale or transportation of intoxicating liquors within...the United States...for beverage purposes...." was ratified in 1919 and took effect one year later. The University Club made the decision to divest itself of the contents of its wine cellar and other liquors through sale to the membership. Members were invited to state how many bottles, and of what, they wished to purchase. Not surprisingly, the offers to purchase greatly exceeded the inventory on hand. As a result, many members had to make do with a single bottle of wine, rather than a whole case. This does not mean that the Club was entirely "dry" during Prohibition, as the presence of small lockers behind the paneling of what is now the Tap Room indicate a provision for housing some private stock.

In the four years leading up to Prohibition, the Club reported an average annual revenue of $49,400 attributable to wine and liquor. In 1919, this figure jumped to $121,413, which no doubt reflects the sale of the Club's inventory. The next year, there was a healthy $89,461 in wine and liquor-related revenue. However, in 1921, with Prohibition in force, "beverages" only accounted for $10,640 in revenue (which presumably includes soft drinks, as well as "set ups" for members arriving with flasks in their pockets). During the remainder of the decade, annual "beverage" revenue remained in the $10,000 range. (In 1934, the first year after the repeal of the Eighteenth Amendment, the Club reported beverage revenue of $23,556.)

The Great Depression caused a precipitous decline in the number of Club members (see foldout graph, following page 18). The Club was forced to reduce expenditures in the face of a reduction in dues income, and lesser usage. During 1932, the coal-fired furnaces in the clubhouse were converted to burn oil, resulting in a cost savings. In January 1932, all staff salaries were reduced by 10 percent, and in November of that same year, there was a further 10 percent reduction, except for those employees whose salary was less than $100 a month. Four years later, after a strike by the "hallboys" (known today as hall attendants), that group was given a 5 percent increase.

In 1934, desperate for finances and out of options, the Council borrowed $20,000 of unspent income from the A. Barton Hepburn Library Fund for general operating expenses. This was done over the protest of the Library Committee, which maintained the loan violated the terms of the Hepburn gift. As Mark Kiley, then Club librarian, wrote many years later, "[t]he library was the only department in the club that had any ready money." By 1942, the loan had been repaid in full, with interest.

> This does not mean that the Club was entirely "dry" during Prohibition, as the presence of small lockers behind the paneling of what is now the Tap Room indicate a provision for housing some private stock.

These steps helped the Club to remain solvent. The financial reports for the decade indicate that only in 1935 did the Club have a loss. In other years, the receipt of entrance fees and life membership dues helped keep the Club in the black. Fortunately, as members were resigning (or being expelled for non-payment of dues), others were joining the Club. In 1936, the Club made improvements costing $120,000 to the building that were funded through issuing ten-year notes with a 4 percent coupon, subscribed to by members. By fiscal 1937, the Club reported an operating surplus of $48,978 and in the following year, a surplus of $50,609. In his letter to the membership in 1939, President Walter Hope paid tribute to the response of the membership to the request for voluntary contributions. He reported that "over seventy-six percent of the members responded favorably and eighty-two Life Members, who were under no obligation to pay dues," made contributions. Once again, the members who are the lifeblood of the Club, demonstrated their loyalty by ensuring the Club's solvency.

Inviting the Ladies

Various Dates

THE UNIVERSITY CLUB
NEW YORK

A DINNER

TO WHICH LADIES MAY BE INVITED WILL BE

HELD IN THE MAIN DINING ROOM OF

THE CLUB HOUSE ON

SUNDAY EVENING, DECEMBER 20, 1936,

AT 8 O'CLOCK

THE GUESTS OF THE CLUB THAT EVENING WILL BE

THE D'OYLY CARTE OPERA COMPANY

OF LONDON

[OVER]

550

The Dinner will begin promptly at 8 P.M. Aperitifs and Cocktails will be served in the Grill Room at 7.30 P.M. The rules for the admission of guests will be suspended that evening and both ladies and gentlemen may be invited. In view of the limited capacity each member will be restricted to one guest and it is urged that tables of eight or ten be arranged jointly with other members. The dinner will be $5.00 per person which will include aperitifs and cocktails.

If you expect to attend please return the enclosed card with the name of your guest, if any. Reservations will be made only in the order of their receipt through ... Members will be prompt...

Invitation and menu for the first evening event to which ladies were invited.

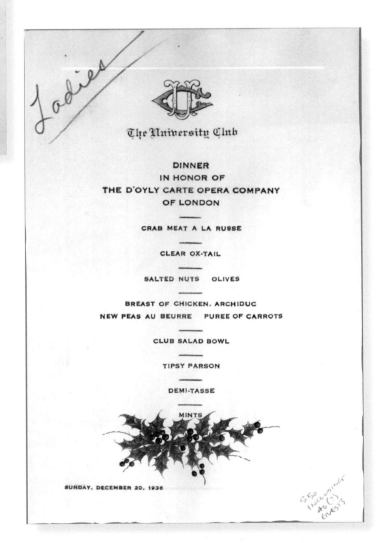

The University Club

DINNER
IN HONOR OF
THE D'OYLY CARTE OPERA COMPANY
OF LONDON

CRAB MEAT A LA RUSSE

CLEAR OX-TAIL

SALTED NUTS   OLIVES

BREAST OF CHICKEN, ARCHIDUC
NEW PEAS AU BEURRE   PUREE OF CARROTS

CLUB SALAD BOWL

TIPSY PARSON

DEMI-TASSE

MINTS

SUNDAY, DECEMBER 20, 1936

Elihu Root

Elihu Root

Address by former Secretary of State Elihu Root to The University Club's seventieth anniversary dinner, February 15, 1935:

Fellow members of The University Club: I am much pleased that you should link my ninetieth birthday with the seventieth anniversary of the Club in this kindly way. There must be a very small group surviving from those young fellows who in May, 1879, undertook to revive and reorganize The University Club, with the good results that we can observe today. We were young, energetic, hopeful, and I dare say we were nearly as superior to the generation preceding us as the youngest alumni of the present time are superior to us.

In our reorganization meeting fifty-five years ago, we happily and gaily devoted the entire night to thrashing out the details of reorganization and electing the new officers. I am forced to realize that as Bismarck used up his allowance of champagne too early in life, I for one have used up my allowance of nights out, and must go early to bed.

Do not think the young men of that time fully appreciated how much of an institution they were building up. Seventy years ago, the institutions for what we call higher education in this country stood practically each by itself alone, having no points of contact and little influence one upon another.

There was but little thought of a system of liberal education. In the great success of this Club and the many university clubs that have followed this example throughout the country, the college and university alumni of the country have practically formed a university inter-relation, along with which has come naturally a more organized relation between universities and colleges themselves, stimulating and enlarging effort and understanding, and we can now see emerging something like a system of liberal education throughout the country. How important that is, one need not argue. In the vast complexity and speed of modern life, political, financial and industrial conditions, with the causes that affect them and the results that flow from them, tend to pass beyond the competency of the uninstructed to understand or control.

We greatly need trained and intelligent leadership in public and private discussion. The ignorance of liberty experienced is readily accompanied by intolerance and narrowness of view. The continued success of democracy must meet the increased complexity, one of social organization and afford a force of greater intelligence, vision, breadth or view and capacity to apply the lessons of human life in the past to human life in the present. That is the true objective of a liberal education. Liberal spirit means love of liberty for oneself and equal love of liberty for others. It means the kindly consideration and sympathy with others that makes for peace and order. It means an appeal to all that is fine and noble in the history of our race, and happy, inescapable lessons that have been drawn by the nature of man, by the highest intelligence and noblest characters of human history, and it means the will to apply those lessons to promote and enlarge the progress of mankind without sacrificing the fundamental principles on which order and liberty depend.

The existence of this Club declares the essential unity of the venerable and cherished institutions upon which rest so great a service for human welfare.

Elihu Root (1845–1937) was a member of The University Club from 1879 to 1937. A lawyer by training, he served as Secretary of War from 1899 to 1904, Secretary of State from 1905 to 1909, and as a U.S. Senator from New York from 1909 to 1915. In 1912, he was awarded the Nobel Peace Prize for his work in improving relations between the United States and Latin American countries, negotiating an agreement with Japan, and in the field of international arbitration.

70th Anniversary Celebration

1865 – 1935

1865 **UC** 1935

THE UNIVERSITY CLUB

The year nineteen hundred thirty-five marks the Seventieth Anniversary of the Founding of the University Club. On February fifteenth of this year

THE HONORABLE ELIHU ROOT

will celebrate his ninetieth birthday and will be completing his fifty-fifth year as a member of the Club.

In honor of our beloved fellow-member and in celebration of the occasion, a meeting will be held at the Clubhouse on the evening of February fifteenth at half past eight o'clock.

Mr. George W. Wickersham, Mr. John W. Davis and Mr. Robert Bridges will speak.

At the conclusion of the ceremonies supper will be served.

Printed and mailed to entire membership by Malcolm & Hayes, Ptrs. 137 E. 43d St. N.Y.C.

In the end, Root's age prevented his making a personal appearance.
He delivered his talk via a wireless connection.

George Washington by Gilbert Stuart

Various Dates

The exhibition of portraits of George Washington by Gilbert Stuart included the Club's canvas, hanging today in the Percy Douglas Reading Room. The exhibit later travelled to the Colony Club.

Gilbert Stuart, 1758–1828
George Washington

Oil on canvas
28½ x 23½ inches

An Intimate Glimpse

1922

An irreverent view of the Club from the old *Life* magazine

Concert Programs

Various Dates

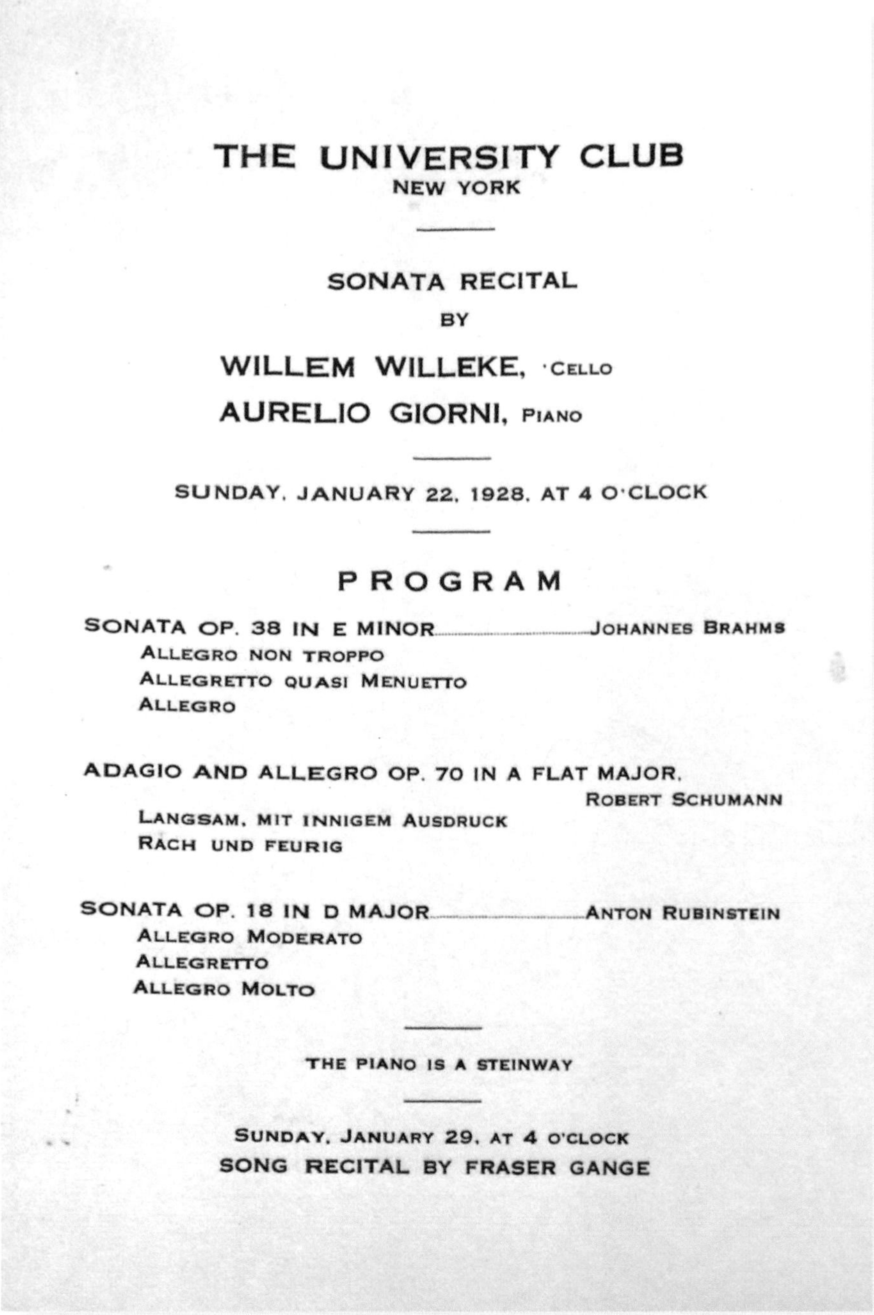

THE UNIVERSITY CLUB
NEW YORK

———

SONATA RECITAL
BY
WILLEM WILLEKE, ʼCELLO
AURELIO GIORNI, PIANO

———

SUNDAY, JANUARY 22, 1928, AT 4 OʼCLOCK

———

PROGRAM

SONATA OP. 38 IN E MINOR...................JOHANNES BRAHMS
    ALLEGRO NON TROPPO
    ALLEGRETTO QUASI MENUETTO
    ALLEGRO

ADAGIO AND ALLEGRO OP. 70 IN A FLAT MAJOR,
                           ROBERT SCHUMANN
    LANGSAM, MIT INNIGEM AUSDRUCK
    RACH UND FEURIG

SONATA OP. 18 IN D MAJOR...................ANTON RUBINSTEIN
    ALLEGRO MODERATO
    ALLEGRETTO
    ALLEGRO MOLTO

———

THE PIANO IS A STEINWAY

———

SUNDAY, JANUARY 29, AT 4 OʼCLOCK
SONG RECITAL BY FRASER GANGE

For a number of years, the Club offered concerts on Sunday afternoons. These are a few of the invitations. Note that ladies could be invited to the 1933 concert.

CONCERT

THE UNIVERSITY CLUB
NEW YORK

HERBERT WITHERSPOON, BASS

ERNEST HUTCHESON, PIANIST

FRANCIS MOORE, ACCOMPANIST

PROGRAM

I.

A. HEAR ME, YE WINDS AND WAVES................HANDEL
   FROM THE OPERA "JULIUS CAESAR"
B. NON PIU' ANDRAI.................................MOZART
   FROM THE OPERA "LE NOZZE DI FIGARO"
C. THE LINDEN TREE................................SCHUBERT
D. THE TWO GRENADIERS...........................SCHUMANN

II.

A. NOCTURNE IN F MAJOR...........................CHOPIN
B. FANTASIE IN F MINOR, OP. 49...................CHOPIN

III.

A. BACIAMI ....TOSTI
B. UN RAMO DI ROSA.................................BILLI
C. SI VOUS VOULIEZ BIEN..........................MASSENET
D. CHANSON ESPAGNOLE.............................GEORGES

IV.

A. ROMANCE, OP. 28, NO. 2.........................SCHUMANN
B. ETUDE DE CONCERT IN F MINOR....................LISZT
C. SCHERZO FROM "A MIDSUMMER'S NIGHT'S
   DREAM"...........................MENDELSSOHN-HUTCHESON
D. RIDE OF THE VALKYRIES............WAGNER-HUTCHESON

V.

A. MOTHER O' MINE (KIPLING)........................TOURS
   EYES OF BLUE....................................ORTH
B. THE AULD FISHER.........................OLD SCOTH SONG
   AFTON WATER............................OLD SCOTH SONG
C. BLACK SHEELA OF THE SILVER EYE....OLD IRISH JIG
D. DANNY DEEVER (KIPLING)......................DAMROSCH

STEINWAY PIANO

SUNDAY AFTERNOON, FEBRUARY 6, AT 4 O'CLOCK

CONCERT BY THE NEW YORK TRIO (VIOLIN, CELLO AND PIANO),
SUNDAY AFTERNOON, FEBRUARY 27, AT 4 O'CLOCK

The University Club
NEW YORK

Brahms and Debussy Recital

On Sunday, March 5, 1933

beginning promptly at 3:30 o'clock, the *Manhattan String Quartet* will present at the University Club the following programme:

Quartet A minor, Opus 51 No. 2 . *Brahms*

Quartet G minor (1893) . . . . . *Debussy*

The Brahms quartet will be played in commemoration of the centenary of the birth of Brahms.

Members of the Club attending the concert will have the privilege of bringing ladies, whom the Entertainment Committee has pleasure in inviting. The Council has suspended for the afternoon the application of the second clause of Rule XXII, with respect to the main floor of the Club. Other floors will be restricted as usual to the use of members.

At the close of the concert tea will be served at a nominal charge.

THE ENTERTAINMENT COMMITTEE

February 23, 1933

Poet Laureate Invitation

1933

> # The University Club
> ### NEW YORK
>
> ## Saturday Luncheon—John Masefield
>
> On Saturday, February 18, 1933
> the Club will have as its guest at luncheon
> *Mr. John Masefield*, Poet Laureate of England.
> Mr. Thomas W. Lamont, president of
> the Club, will preside.
> Luncheon will be served as usual at 1:30
> o'clock, and the speaking will begin at 2:15.
> If you will be present at the luncheon,
> please mark the enclosed card and return it
> as promptly as possible to
>
> THE ENTERTAINMENT COMMITTEE
>
> 1 West 54th Street
> New York
> February 9, 1933

John Masefield, Poet Laureate of England from 1930 to 1967, was a playwright and fiction writer, as well as a poet. His poems include "Sea Fever" and "Cargoes." He also wrote some verse to honor the tercentenary of Harvard College in 1936.

Italian Foreign Minister Invitation

1936

The University Club
NEW YORK

———

LUNCHEON

SATURDAY, JANUARY 4, 1936
PROMPTLY AT ONE-THIRTY O'CLOCK

The Club will have as its guest

HIS EXCELLENCY COUNT CARLO SFORZA
Former Minister of Foreign Affairs of Italy

who will speak on

PRESENT PROBLEMS IN EUROPE

Count Sforza was Minister of Foreign Relations prior to the existing regime and has been Italian Ambassador to France and Minister to China. He is a member of the European Council of the Carnegie Endowment for International Peace.

Speaking will begin at two-fifteen.

If you will be present, please sign and return the enclosed card.

The Entertainment Committee.

One can only speculate what this gentleman, from the pre-Mussolini government, had to say about rising tensions in Europe.

First Club Bulletin

1934

THE UNIVERSITY CLUB

NEW YORK

MEMBERS' BULLETIN
JUNE, 1934

FIFTH AVENUE AND 54TH STREET, NEW YORK

within the period from October 31, 1929, to March 31, 1934, shall be exempt from the payment of entrance fees in the event of re-election of such former member to membership in the Club prior to December 1, 1934.

By now practically every former member, however remote, who resigned within the period named should have received formal notification of the opportunity thus opened to him. Present members who may want to further the re-election of former members can obtain information from the Club Office as to the formalities to be followed.

THE NEW LOUNGE

The new lounge on the second floor on the Fifty-fourth Street side, which was constructed in anticipation of repeal, was opened immediately after repeal became effective. It has proved to be one of the most attractive rooms in the Club. Very recently an air-conditioning and cooling system was put into operation, thereby adapting the lounge to summer use.

THE SWIMMING POOL AND TURKISH BATHS

Another feature of the Club, one which has always had special use during the summer, is the pool. It has a capacity of about 38,000 gallons and receives over 7,500 gallons of fresh water every day. Water comes through a circulating system with continuous filter-

ing, and is subjected to an ultra-violet ray sterilizer which assures sanitary pool conditions of the highest standard. The pool and Turkish baths are open daily from 7 a.m. to 8 p.m., except on Sundays, when the closing hour is 7 o'clock. The range of charges is:

Electric light cabinet	$1.25
Electric light cabinet and rub	1.50
Shower and plunge	.50
Shower and plunge, hot or steam room	.75
Hot room	1.00
Hot room and rub	1.25

ROOMS BY THE MONTH OR FOR TRANSIENTS

Members who close their apartments or houses during the summer and non-residents who are in New York overnight will find the Club's sleeping rooms convenient and attractive. Ordinarily advance reservations are not necessary, but to be on the safe side it is well to notify the Club's Office a day or so before arrival. All rooms are equipped with bath, and the rental includes valet, local telephone and other services.

NEW SQUASH COURTS

During the summer extensive changes will be made in the squash courts. Upon completion it is expected that the Club will have quite the best facilities for squash racquets in the metropolitan area.

Special Dinner Menu

1936

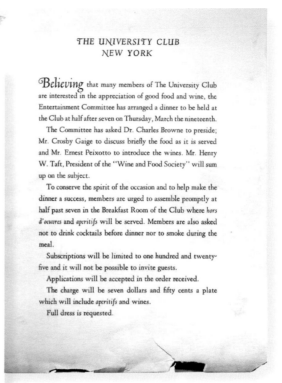

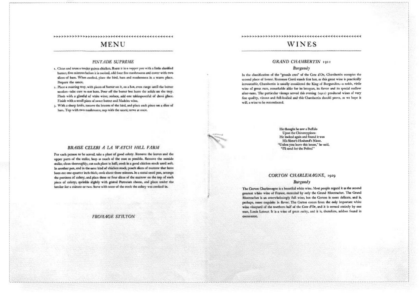

A grand dinner hosted by the Club

Winslow Homer Exhibit

1938

THE UNIVERSITY CLUB
NEW YORK

AN EXHIBITION
of
DRAWINGS
by
WINSLOW HOMER

Lent by

The Cooper Union Museum

for the Arts of Decoration

April 9 through 23

1938

NOTE

The University Club is privileged to show the drawings of one of the greatest of American artists, Winslow Homer, through the generosity of the Directors of the Cooper Union Museum. The collection from which the thirty-one sketches have been selected numbers nearly three hundred, as well as twenty-two oil paintings. These were given to the Cooper Union by Mrs. Charles Savage Homer and the late Mr. Homer, and by the late Charles W. Gould.

The group exhibited dates from 1861, when the artist was making drawings for reproduction in Harper's Weekly, during the War of the Rebellion, to 1895; and they show the different phases of his interests especially his most absorbing and masterful art in depicting the ocean. They show, also, for those who are interested in technicalities, the skill with which he handled various media through his "first tinting with watercolor of substantial line drawings, on to the unhesitating strength of his later watercolorings, in which the expressive brush seems almost to have been guided by a Chinese calligrapher."

1	"Dixie" (the 'Songs of the War').	1861
	Pencil on paper with washes of water-color.	
2	Infantry Marching.	1862
	Pencil on tracing paper.	
3	Soldiers in a Field.	1862
	Pencil on paper.	
4	Four Soldiers' Heads.	1863
	Charcoal on yellow paper.	
5	Soldier on horseback.	1863
	Black crayon on paper.	
6	Soldier on horseback, with upraised sword.	1862
	Black crayon on paper.	
7	Wounded Soldier given water.	1864
	Charcoal and white crayon on green paper.	
8	Four sketches of soldiers.	1864
	Charcoal and white crayon on brown paper.	
9	Drummer seen from back.	1864
	Charcoal and white crayon on blue-green paper.	
10	Recumbent figure of a man.	1865
	Black and white crayon on gray-brown paper.	
11	Soldier loading a rifle.	1865
	Charcoal and white crayon on green paper.	
12	Child in a sunbonnet asleep.	1878
	Pencil and Chinese white on gray-green paper.	
13	Woman lying in a field.	1878
	Charcoal on cardboard.	
14	Schooner with dinghy.	1880
	Pencil on gray paper.	
15	Two schooners, one with broken spinacker and yawl.	1880
	Pencil with Chinese white on neutral yellow paper.	
16	Low rocky seacoast.	1880
	Charcoal and white crayon on gray paper.	
17	Watching a storm at Tynemouth.	1881
	Charcoal and white crayon on paper.	

18	The Rescue.	1881
	Charcoal, black water-color and Chinese white on paper.	
19	"The Life Line", sketch for painting.	1882-83
	Charcoal on paper.	
20	Banks Fishmen, or Herring Nets.	1885
	Black and white crayon on green paper.	
21	Hillside with roots of trees.	1885
	Charcoal and Chinese white on gray paper.	
22	Rocky shore with surf.	1885
	Charcoal with white crayon on gray paper.	
23	Morro Castle, Santiago de Cuba. Sketch for painting.	1886
	Pencil and white crayon on gray paper.	
24	"The Gulf Stream", Study for painting.	1886
	Water-color on cold pressed paper.	
25	Ocean swells.	1890
	Charcoal and white crayon on gray paper.	
26	Clouded sky, flat sea, shore background.	1890
	Pencil and water-color on paper.	
27	Landscape with morning haze.	1890
	Pencil and water-color on paper.	
28	Ocean from a cliff.	1894
	Water-color on paper.	
29	Mountain lake in hills.	1895
	Pencil and water-color on paper.	
30	Fisherman in the Adirondacks.	1895
	Pencil, black wash and Chinese white on gray paper.	
31	"The Look out – All's Well." Studies for painting.	1895-96
	Charcoal on paper.	
32	Two-masted Schooner with dory.	1894
	Water-color on paper.	

Holding exhibits of borrowed works of art was a custom of the Club's for a number of years. This is the program for one such event.

Presidents Dinner

1939

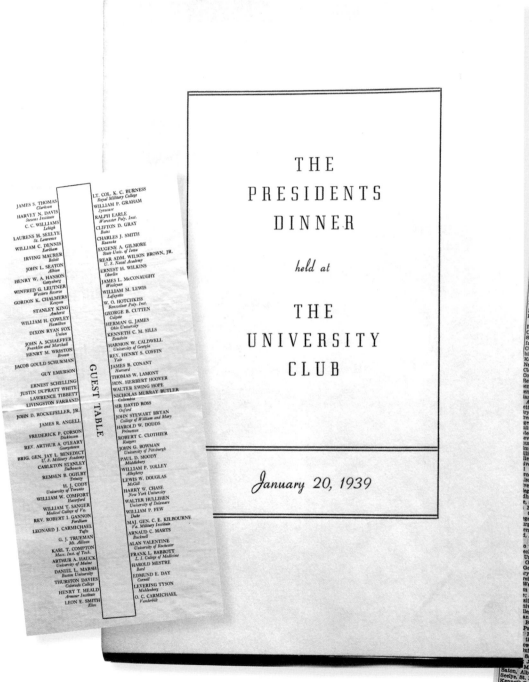

In 1939, the Club hosted a dinner for seventy-two presidents of colleges and universities. The institutions were all ones whose alumni were represented in the membership, and the presidents were seated at the head table in the order of the founding of their institution. Ernest Schelling, pianist, and Lawrence Tibbett, baritone, provided entertainment. President Nicholas Murray Butler of Columbia University and Thomas Lamont, a prominent financier and former president of the Club, gave addresses. Later, their addresses were printed in a booklet distributed to the membership. Subsequent dinners for college and university presidents were held in 1941 and 1947.

College Hall Night

1939

THE UNIVERSITY CLUB

FIRST COLLEGE HALL NIGHT
OF THE SEASON

FRIDAY EVENING NOVEMBER 3rd, 1939
9 to 12 P. M.

THIS IS THE NIGHT BEFORE

HARVARD vs. PRINCETON at PRINCETON
YALE vs. DARTMOUTH at NEW HAVEN
CORNELL vs. COLUMBIA at ITHACA
N. Y. U. vs. LAFAYETTE at NEW YORK
NOTRE DAME vs. ARMY at NEW YORK

Therefore, this first College Hall Night, is designated

NON-RESIDENT NIGHT

BEER - SANDWICHES - SONGS

THE UNIVERSITY GLEE CLUB
will be among our guests and help in
OLD SONGS

Mr. Richards Vidmer, well known sports writer of the Herald-Tribune and others will be guests.

All members are urged to make this a real Club Night. Come in the late afternoon, dine at the club and stay for Non-Resident Night.

Our new President, Mr. Philip M. Brett, is one of the charter members of the University Glee Club.

Because of the tremendous success of the club parties in College Hall last year, it is planned to hold one each month this winter.

Those members expecting to dine at the club November 3 are requested to sign the enclosed card so the House Committee may make adequate arrangements.

The charge for the party in College Hall will be one dollar and tickets may be obtained any time at the club office or at the door of College Hall.

An invitation to a typical College Hall event of the era

The invitation to the first event in what we now know as College Hall, but was previously the Billiard Room. To accommodate the event, all billiard and pool tables were removed, never to return.

British Ambassador / Council Dinner Menu

1939 – 1940

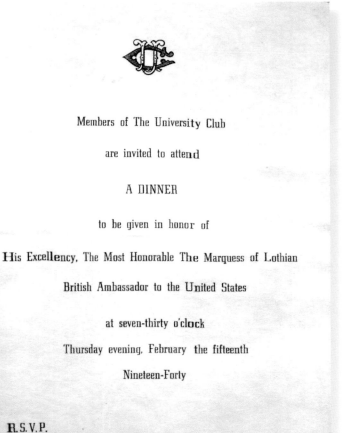

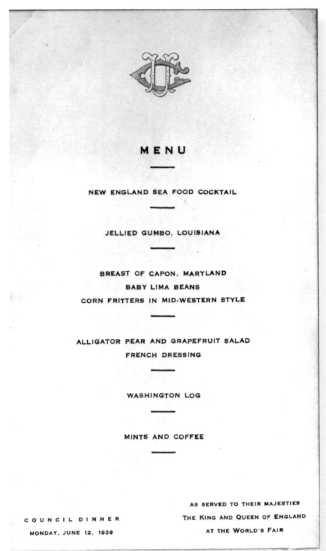

Left: The ambassador came to the Club during a lull in World War II. After crushing Poland in the fall of 1939, the Germans waited until spring 1940 before invading France, Belgium and the Netherlands. This would lead to the evacuation of the British army through Dunkirk. **Right:** A Council dinner menu from 1939

First Library Dinner

1939

ROMANCE
Lunette at east end of the University Club Library

THE UNIVERSITY CLUB

NEW YORK

March 4, 1939

CLUB DINNER

On Friday evening, March 17th, a dinner sponsored by the Library Committee will be held in College Hall. It is suggested that members take advantage of this occasion to invite as their guests men who will be particularly interested in this literary dinner.

Professor William Lyon Phelps has accepted our invitation to be the special guest of the evening and speak. We also expect to have with us other men prominent in literature.

It will be appreciated by the Dinner Committee if members respond as promptly as possible. Members may be seated together as requested if seating preferences reach the Club office not later than March 13th.

The subscription will be $3.50 per plate and will be charged to house accounts. Dinner will be served promptly at eight o'clock. Cocktails will be served in the Grill Room at 7:30 o'clock. Members will sign for cocktails during the reception and also for beverages ordered at the dinner.

This is the first dinner ever held in the Club under the auspices of the Committee which is responsible for the remarkable work being done in the Library of which we are all so proud. It is hoped there will be a large attendance of members and guests at this dinner which we believe will be one of the most interesting events of the Club year.

Entertainment Committee

Menu for the first dinner held under the auspices of the Library Committee on March 17, 1939, in College Hall. The guest of honor was William Lyon Phelps, Professor of English Literature at Yale, and a specialist in modern novels. The dinner cost $3.50, exclusive of beverages.

Letter Seeking New Members

The University Club
1 West 54th Street
New York City

We are writing you and some other members of The University Club who we know are particularly interested in the Club's welfare.

Considering present conditions the Club is in an unusually healthy situation due largely to the energy and enterprise of Mr. Hope through his presidency and the continuation of this through the presidency of Mr. Brett. Mr. Clarke came into the chairmanship of the House Committee about two and a half years ago and has done one of the best jobs ever done in the Club and the Entertainment Committee has never been more active or successful. Economies have been made with at the same time better service and more activity in the Club than we have had for years.

The outlook for this winter season is particularly bright and the Entertainment Committee has already planned not only the usual Saturday Luncheons and College Hall parties but in addition probably three ladies dinners with outstanding programs. For October 25th we are already assured of an attendance to our capacity. On November 14th we are going to celebrate our 75th Anniversary with a Club dinner of major importance.

The Clubhouse has been done over from top to bottom which included major expenditures in the Baths, the installation of College Hall and the air conditioning of the Grill Room.

While all of this has been accomplished we have still not met the one major issue that has been before us for several years. Mr. Hope was induced to carry on as president for two years after he wished to retire, with the understanding that he would personally be relieved of the membership problem and that it would be taken over by the members of the Council. We have worked with Mr. Hope and are now cooperating with Mr. Brett but we feel that the active Club membership owes it to these two men who have done so much for us to meet the membership situation and meet it now. No one man and no committee can do the job. Our total membership today is about 2900 including the various classes of membership. We are carrying on but in these times we must expect a certain number of resignations. Also, our average age of membership, as we all know, is high with a corresponding high loss through deaths. It has been most gratifying the way younger men have been coming in but we need more and we feel that now is the time to face the membership problem instead of waiting until a time when it is too late. In comparison with many other clubs, The University Club has a real reason for being. We do not want to face an increase in dues. We should not increase our house charges. We should in these times try to give more rather than less service to our members.

This situation can be met if we have an increase in membership of 500 beyond the regular flow of new members which we hope will offset those who resign or die.

At our 75th Anniversary dinner on November 14th, we would like to give Mr. Brett the pleasure of being able to announce that we have elected or there are on the waiting list or on the way to proposal these 500 new members.

If you and each of the others of the selected group to whom we are writing will give one evening to the Club, going over the names of those with whom you are associated either socially or in business, we are sure that each of you can find at least one man fully qualified who would welcome the opportunity of Club election. While we need members, we will not let down in any way in our qualifications.

The officers of the Club and others who are working officially for the Club in various capacities have their hands full with Club business, so we have taken it upon ourselves to present this case to a selected group of our members asking their serious consideration of the Club's need at this time.

This is not a cry of distress. We are simply asking individual support for one of the most successful clubs in the city, looking forward to greater things in the future. If you will write a note to Mr. Robert W. Carle at 153 Water Street (Telephone WH 3-3730) telling him that you will try and put up at least one good member within the next month, you will not only be helping your Club but you will immeasurably cheer Mr. Brett and his associates who are doing so much.

The facilities of the Club office are at your disposal and if you will telephone Mr. Day Manson, Circle 7-2100, or write him, he will furnish membership application blanks and be of any help he possibly can in qualifying your candidate.

Yours sincerely,

Robert W. Carle

E. W. Debevoise

W. E. S. Griswold

Ernest Iselin

L. S. Rockefeller

Earle S. Thompson

This letter seeking new members for the Club was signed by two future Club presidents, Eli Whitney Debevoise and Earle S. Thompson.

Celebrating Philip Brett, Club President

1941

DINNER IN HONOR OF

PHILIP M. BRETT

MAY 8, 1941

When Philip Brett stepped down as president of the Club, he was fêted at a dinner, which included preparation of this newsletter.

Armed Forces Speakers

1941

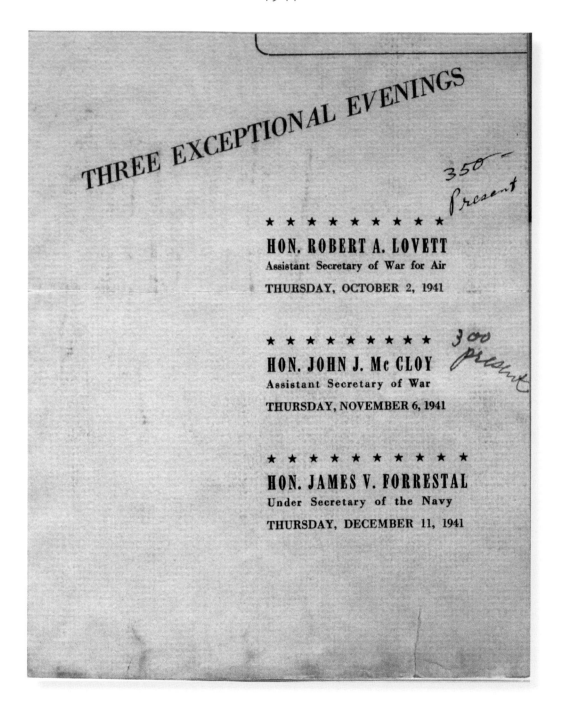

In a departure from the usual practice of inviting speakers on Saturday, three officials were invited on Thursday evenings. Because of the attack on Pearl Harbor, Secretary Forrestal cancelled.

Club Entertainment

1942

The University Club of New York

presents

The Blue Hill Troupe

at a

Gilbert and Sullivan Dinner

on

Sunday evening, March Eighth

Nineteen hundred and forty-two

at Eight o'clock

R.S.V.P.   Cocktails at Seven-fifteen
Enclosed Card   See inside page for details

376 present   *Dec. 13, 1942*

The Pleasure of Your Company is Requested
at a
Dinner - Musicale
presenting
Miss Lucielle Browning
Miss Annamary Dickey
Mr. John Dudley
Mr. Arthur Kent
of the
Metropolitan Opera Company
to be held at
The University Club
on
Sunday evening, December thirteenth
Nineteen Hundred and Forty-two
at Eight O'clock

R.S.V.P.   Cocktails at seven-thirty
Enclosed Card   See inside page for details

Two Sunday evening concerts held in 1942

First Dinner Dance

1940

University Club Ends Tradition. Permits Dance

Event To Be Held Tonight to Shatter 75-Year Policy of Sanctuary for Men

The University Club, at 1 West Fifty-fourth Street, founded seventy-five years ago as a male sanctuary for college and university graduates, will break with tradition tonight when, for the first time in its history, it will hold a dance, which some 150 couples are expected to attend.

This will not be the first time that women have been permitted in the club. About two years ago the bars were let down to allow their presence at Sunday evening suppers and at ladies' day, held twice a year. But it will be the first time that they will invade the club in furs and frills for a dance and the first time that the astonished walls will act as sounding boards for such tunes as "Beat Me Daddy, Eight to the Bar."

The dinner dance will start at 8 p. m. and end about 1 a. m. The music will be supplied by Joe Moss and his orchestra. The affair has been arranged by the activities committee and presumably has the approval of the club's officers, Philip M. Brett, president; Thomas M. Debevoise, vice-president; Whitney Darrow, secretary, and S. Sloan Colt, treasurer.

"The dance is for the regular members of the club," a spokesman said last night. "The members may bring their wives or young women friends and may also ask another couple to come along. It is the first time in the club's history that such an affair has been arranged, and we cannot say if it will be the last as well as the first time or if other dances will follow."

It was not until two years ago that women were permitted within the club, where the thick and imposing walls had formed for years a male refuge for such notables as Chauncey M. Depew, Winston Churchill, J. P. Morgan, Thomas W. Lamont, Harry Payne Whitney and John W. Davis. No sound of feminine voices ever penetrated that thick-carpeted peace, nor did any saxophones sob of unrequited love.

The University Club traces its ideology back to the Mermaid Tavern of Elizabethan gentlemen, the Rota Club, where Milton held forth on the politics of the day and the Atheneum Club, regarded as the first such organization in which education was a condition of membership. The club was established by a group of young Yale graduates who took to meeting in New York after the Civil War.

It started in 1865 with a membership of 112, and its first club rooms were small houses in East Tenth Street and at 9 Brevoort Place. In 1879 the club was reorganized and moved its quarters to a new building on the southwest corner of Fifth Avenue and Thirty-fifth Street. Thence it moved to Madison Avenue and Twenty-sixth Street, for a ten-year period. Then the site of old St. Luke's Hospital, on the northwest corner of Fifth Avenue and Fifty-fourth Street, was purchased, and there the club now stands.

And in all these years of movement and growth it remained tenaciously, stubbornly, aggressively male.

In 1940, the *New York Herald Tribune* took humorous note of the Club's first-ever dinner dance.

Event Invitations

1943 and 1944

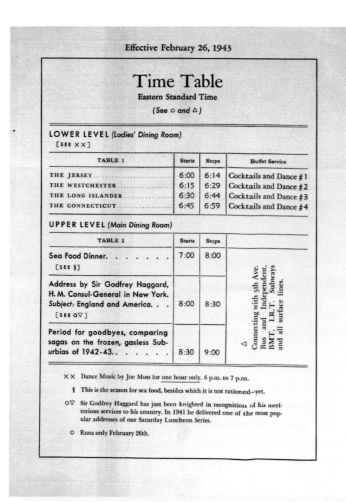

Effective February 26, 1943

Time Table
Eastern Standard Time
(See ○ and △)

LOWER LEVEL (Ladies' Dining Room)
[SEE ××]

TABLE 1	Starts	Stops	Buffet Service
THE JERSEY	6:00	6:14	Cocktails and Dance #1
THE WESTCHESTER	6:15	6:29	Cocktails and Dance #2
THE LONG ISLANDER	6:30	6:44	Cocktails and Dance #3
THE CONNECTICUT	6:45	6:59	Cocktails and Dance #4

UPPER LEVEL (Main Dining Room)

TABLE 2	Starts	Stops	
Sea Food Dinner. . . . . . . [SEE §]	7:00	8:00	
Address by Sir Godfrey Haggard, H. M. Consul-General in New York. Subject: England and America. . . [SEE ○▽]	8:00	8:30	△ Connecting with 5th Ave. Bus and Independent, BMT, I.R.T. Subways and all surface lines.
Period for goodbyes, comparing sagas on the frozen, gasless Suburbias of 1942-43..	8:30	9:00	

×× Dance Music by Joe Moss for one hour only. 6 p.m. to 7 p.m.

§ This is the season for sea food, besides which it is not rationed—yet.

○▽ Sir Godfrey Haggard has just been knighted in recognition of his meritorious services to his country. In 1941 he delivered one of the most popular addresses of our Saturday Luncheon Series.

○ Runs only February 26th.

≈≈≈≈≈≈≈≈≈≈≈≈≈≈≈≈≈≈≈≈≈≈

The University Club
FIFTH ANNUAL DINNER DANCE
DECEMBER 8, 1944

•

LEAP-YEAR AND CUTTING-IN FEATURES

Ladies, this is Leap Year.
For twenty-three days more—
You have the stag's full privilege
To flit about the floor
Selecting partners here and there,
Rejoicing in their dancing,
Leaving them when music stops
And after others prancing.

To stimulate the shy or coy
And carry out this notion
Each table hostess has a toy
Which must be kept in motion.
A lady who receives a monkey
Playing on two sticks
Must quickly swap it for a man.
(Beware his monkey tricks.)

Then to ensure that diffidence,
Or other manly traits,
Won't cause each gentleman to sit
And stare at empty plates,
Each table's host should take the lead,
With gun, to do his duty,
Exhorting friends to go and dance
By trading arms for beauty.

Now, gentlemen and ladies, please,
If face or form you fancy
Of fleeting strangers quite unknown,
Don't act like a "Miss Nancy".
Step right up and cut right in.
Don't hesitate or vary.
Presentations are "de trop";
You do the necessary.

CLUB ACTIVITIES COMMITTEE

Left: A wartime invitation in the guise of a railroad timetable
Right: By the time of the fifth dinner dance, in 1944, the Club poked fun at itself.

Father and Son Dinner

Various Dates

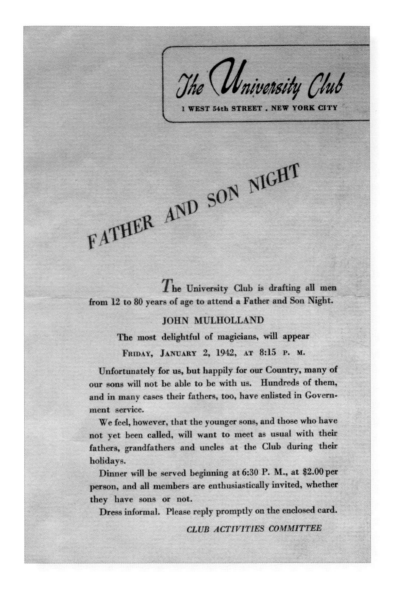

The University Club
1 WEST 54th STREET . NEW YORK CITY

FATHER AND SON NIGHT

The University Club is drafting all men from 12 to 80 years of age to attend a Father and Son Night.

JOHN MULHOLLAND

The most delightful of magicians, will appear
FRIDAY, JANUARY 2, 1942, AT 8:15 P. M.

Unfortunately for us, but happily for our Country, many of our sons will not be able to be with us. Hundreds of them, and in many cases their fathers, too, have enlisted in Government service.

We feel, however, that the younger sons, and those who have not yet been called, will want to meet as usual with their fathers, grandfathers and uncles at the Club during their holidays.

Dinner will be served beginning at 6:30 P. M., at $2.00 per person, and all members are enthusiastically invited, whether they have sons or not.

Dress informal. Please reply promptly on the enclosed card.

CLUB ACTIVITIES COMMITTEE

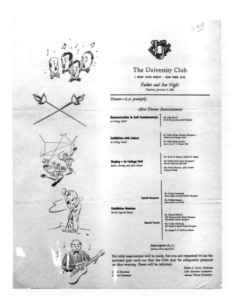

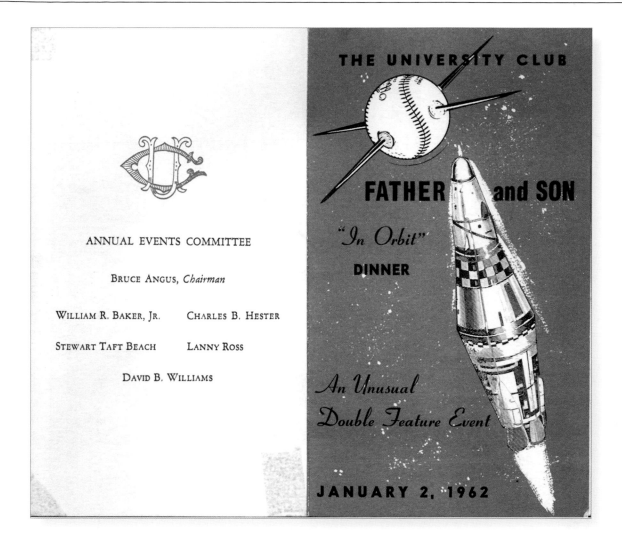

The father and son dinners, later supplemented by father and daughter dinners, were popular events for many years. These are a few of the invitations.

Father and Daughter Dinner

Various Dates

277
11 guests
—
288

The UNIVERSITY CLUB
1 WEST 54th STREET • NEW YORK CITY

FATHER and DAUGHTER DINNER

WEDNESDAY EVENING, APRIL 2nd, 1952

The University Club will hold the Annual Father and Daughter Dinner to which members and their daughters are invited on Wednesday evening, April 2, 1952.

The Dinner will be held in the Main Dining Room which will be followed by an interesting entertainment program including harmony, glamour, laughs and fun!

PRINCETON FRESHMAN GLEE CLUB OCTETTE

Eight Men from Old Nassau

MR. AND MRS. JOHN JAY SCHIEFFELIN
AND
CHARLES BAKER HESTER

Presenting a specialty act

"WHAT EVERY YOUNG GIRL PROBABLY KNOWS"

JAY MARSHALL

? ? ? ? ?

THE COMMITTEE'S SECRET

* * *

Fathers and daughters of all ages are welcome.

DINNER at 7:30 P. M.   SUBSCRIPTION $5.50

(Cocktails may be signed for. Service available in
Main Dining Room at 7 P.M.)

Black Tie Suggested

* * *

No seating arrangements will be made but members are requested to use the enclosed reply card promptly so that the Club may be adequately prepared for this occasion.

ROBERT J. LEWIS—Chairman   ANNUAL EVENTS COMMITTEE

FATHER and DAUGHTER DINNER

Fathers and daughters, permanent or temporary, of all ages are welcome.

UNIVERSITY CLUB ∽ NEW YORK

Friday Evening, March Twentieth 1953

Gala After Dinner Program

THE NIGHT OWLS OF VASSAR
12 Beautiful Girls 12 • Count 'em

GENTLEMEN of the
SOCIETY of ORPHEUS and BACCHUS
Men of Yale • See 'em

The Inimitable Comedienne
ALICE PEARCE, *Sarah Lawrence '40*
with
MARK LAWRENCE, *Princeton '42*
*in a series of songs (?) conceived in the best interests
of insanity and dedicated to the proposition that a
Liberal Arts education need not go utterly to waste.*

Dinner in the Main Dining Room at 7:30 P.M.   SUBSCRIPTION: $9.50

Cocktails may be signed for. Service available
in the Main Dining Room at 7 P.M.

Black Tie Suggested

*No seating arrangements will be made but members are requested
to use the enclosed reply card promptly so that the Club
may be adequately prepared for this occasion.*

ANNUAL EVENTS COMMITTEE

CHARLES B. HESTER, *Chairman*   WILLIAM C. BREED, JR., *Dinner Chairman*

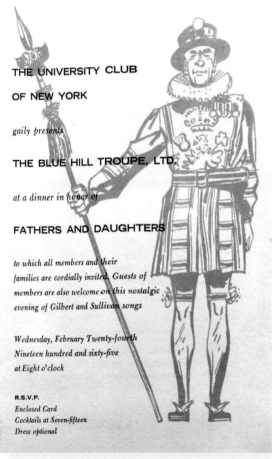

THE UNIVERSITY CLUB

OF NEW YORK

gaily presents

THE BLUE HILL TROUPE, LTD.

at a dinner in honor of

FATHERS AND DAUGHTERS

*to which all members and their
families are cordially invited. Guests of
members are also welcome on this nostalgic
evening of Gilbert and Sullivan songs*

*Wednesday, February Twenty-fourth
Nineteen hundred and sixty-five
at Eight o'clock*

R.S.V.P.
*Enclosed Card
Cocktails at Seven-fifteen
Dress optional*

75th Anniversary Dinner

1940

Menu

Cocktails   *Buffet Russe*

Supreme of Grapefruit au Kirsch

Celery - Olives - Assorted Nuts

Strained Petite Marmite

Napa Valley,   *Broiled Mignon of Beef*
(California)
Cabernet 1934   *String Beans au Gratin*
Inglenook Vineyards
       Pommes Chateau

Epicurean Salad

Anniversary Glacée

Cigars   *Moka*

PHILIP MILLEDOLER BRETT
President of The University Club
PRESIDING

The First Seventy-five Years of
The University Club
in song, play and picture
presented by
GROSVENOR ATTERBURY
assisted by members and friends

CHARLES KULLMAN, *Yale 1928*
Tenor Metropolitan Opera Co.
accompanied on the piano by
FRANK ST. LEGER, *Conductor Metropolitan Opera Co.*

WENDELL L. WILLKIE

University Club Hears Willkie On Anniversary

History of Organization Is Pictured Since Founding 75 Years Ago by Yale Men

The University Club of New York celebrated its seventy-fifth anniversary last night at the clubhouse, 1 West Fifty-fourth Street, with Wendell L. Willkie, a member of the club, the only speaker.

The celebration started with a dinner which was attended by 600 members. The dinner was followed by the presentation of the history of the club and the city for the last seventy-five years by means of lantern slides, songs by the glee club, a one-act play by George E. Brewer Jr., playwright, and a prologue and epilogue by Grosvenor Atterbury, architect.

Everything was for and by the club members, so that nothing said by Mr. Willkie, or Philip M. Brett, president of the club, who introduced him, was for publication.

The one-act play, which had no title, showed a room in the residence of Joseph Kernochan, a noted lawyer of his day, at 145 Second Avenue, where his son, Francis Edward Kernochan, and fourteen other Yale men organized the Red Room Club in 1861, immediately after the younger Kernochan's graduation from Yale. The club received its name from the color of the wall paper.

The time of the play was Jan. 18, 1865, when young Mr. Kernochan and the other sons of Eli were in a benevolent mood and admitted men from Princeton, Harvard and other colleges to their circle. This was the beginning of the University Club. Other Yale men represented in the one-act play, were Frederic Kernochan, a brother of Francis; Franklin MacVeagh, Henry Holt, William C Whitney and Buchanan Winthrop Theodore William Dwight was the club's first president.

Mr. Willkie's speech brought the celebration to a close.

The University Club has occupied four houses since its founding. The first was at 9 Brevoort Place. In 1879 to 1884 the club occupied a house at the corner of Fifth Avenue and Thirty-fifth street. Then the club moved to the former home of Leonard Jerome, at Madison Avenue and Twenty-sixth Street, now the Manhattan Club. Mr. Jerome was the father of Lady Randolph Churchill and the grandfather of Winston Churchill, Prime Minister of Great Britain.

In 1899 the club moved into its present home at 1 West Fifty-fourth Street, which was built under the direction of the architectural firm of McKim, Mead & White. Both Charles F. McKim and Stanford White personally directed the construction of the clubhouse, which is said to be an example of their finest work.

The Club's seventy-fifth anniversary dinner, on December 18, 1940, was written up in the *New York Herald Tribune*.

Cigar Sales

Dec/1920

THE UNIVERSITY CLUB
NEW YORK CITY

THE HOUSE COMMITTEE OFFERS THE FOLLOWING PARTICULARLY
FINE CIGARS AS A SUGGESTION FOR CHRISTMAS GIFTS:

			BOXES OF	PRICE PER 100
HENRY CLAY	PANETELAS SALAMONES	E M	50	$58.00
" "	ELOCUENTES	"	50	42.00
" "	MIKADO	"	10	70.00
" "	CORONA LARGAS	"	50	56.00
VILLAR Y VILLA	ESPECIALS		50	56.00
" "	ENGLISH PERFECTOS (CROP 1914)	B N	50	40.00
" "	NACIONALES	"	50	44.00
" "	SUPERBAS (CROP 1916)		50	53.00
"	SALAMONES EXTRA		100	68.00
MANUEL GARCIA	ALONSO CELESTIALES	E M	50	52.00
" "	" CORNITAS	"	100	29.00
H. DE CABANAS Y CABAJAL	ADORNADOS	"	25	43.00
" "	" INCLITOS		100	54.00
"	" PREMIERS	50 & 100		54.00
LA CORONA	CORONAS	50 & 100		56.00
" "	" LARGAS CROP (1916)		100	58.00
" "	" GRANDES		100	73.00
" "	GLORIOSOS		50	80.00
BELINDA	CREME SELECCION	B N	50	52.00
POR LARRAÑAGA	ORIENTALES	(CROP 1908)	25	56.90
EDEN	SELECCION DEL EDEN		100	46.00
"	OPORTUNOS		25	39.00
BOLIVAR	CORONAS	B N	50	52.00
"	ENGLISH CORONAS		100	56.00
"	CORONAS GRANDES		10	80.00
PEDRO MURIAS	DANTE B N		50	54.00

E. M.—CIGARS MANUFACTURED FOR ENGLISH MARKET.

B N.—BOITE NATURE.

THESE CIGARS HAVE BEEN CONDITIONED IN OUR OWN HUMIDOR
FOR OVER A YEAR UNDER PERFECT CONTROL OF MOISTURE AND
TEMPERATURE.

CARRIAGE AND INSURANCE PREPAID ON OUT OF TOWN ORDERS.

For years, it was the practice of the Club to purchase cigars in bulk and encourage members to buy them for gifts. During the decade of the 1920s, the Club's average annual revenue from the sale of cigars was $100,667.

The Club in World War II

Although the years of the Second World War presented The University Club with a number of challenges, especially in its finances and staffing, by the end of the war, the Club was in a strong position. As in the case of first war, members in the armed forces were excused from paying dues while on active duty, which translated into an annual drop of $30,000 in income. Another financial blow came when a large number of employees left, either because they were drafted or found higher-paying work in war-related industries. Finding qualified people to replace them was not easy; however, the Club managed to maintain most services. In 1943, the House Committee even considered hiring women to operate the elevators, but did not do so.

To keep inflation under control during the war, the U.S. government established the National War Labor Board with authority to approve wage increases, and the Office of Price Administration with similar control over prices. Thus, before the Club could increase prices in the restaurant to reflect higher costs for goods, approval had to be obtained from the federal agency. In 1943, after a number of Club employees joined the Hotel and Club Employees Union, the union petitioned the labor board for a 25 percent increase in pay, which was denied. However, with the approval of the labor board, the Club and the union compromised on a modest increase.

In 1943, the Club's manager, Charles Hynes, resigned and accepted a commission in the navy. Rather than replace him, the Club decided to save his salary and the chairman of the House Committee, H. Edward Bilkey, assumed the direct supervision of the Club's department heads. Once the war was over, Hynes returned and served the Club until 1963.

The Club was very active throughout the war. Membership increased from 3,000 in 1941 to 3,381 in 1945. The Saturday lecture series continued, special

Announcement

The present gasoline shortage will undoubtedly cause many of our members and their families to be in town this summer.

Starting Sunday, July 12th a Buffet Supper will be served every Sunday evening in the Ladies' Dining Room, from six to nine o'clock, at $1.75 per person. Tea and other beverage service will be available at four o'clock.

Our air conditioning insures complete comfort during the hot summer months and it is felt that these informal Sunday evenings will furnish additional enjoyment to our members, their families and friends.

1942

The House Committee

Gasoline rationing during World War II prompted the Club to offer buffet supper on Sunday evenings. This proved so popular that members were asked to limit the number of guests they brought.

events such as the "Books in Wartime" dinner in 1943 were held, as were the customary father and son, and father and daughter, dinners. The squash courts and the baths department (as the fitness center was then called) reported heavy usage. In early 1945, the president, Earle Thompson, reported that it was a record year in terms of usage and the Club's finances. For the second year in a row, the restaurant ran without showing a loss, notwithstanding the obstacles raised by food rationing. The Ladies Dining Room on the ground floor was very popular, so much so that members were asked to limit the number of guests they brought on certain evenings. A number of repairs were made to the clubhouse, including the removal of oil-fired furnaces. From then on, heat was supplied with steam piped into the building. The Club was able to retire a few of the one-year notes subscribed to by members, and to pay down some of the principal of the mortgage.

As a concession to wartime conditions and to encourage people to make use of public transportation, the evening dress code for ladies was relaxed to make wearing of evening (i.e., long) dresses optional. There was no equivalent reduction in the evening dress code for men, however.

In 1946, the Club published *Tribute to the War Records of Our Members,* which gave information about the wartime activities of some 700 members, both in and out of uniform, in both world wars. Each of the eight members killed in action in the Second World War was given a page in the book, and their names were inscribed in the Main Atrium. Of those eight men, two served in the U.S. Army, three in the Navy, two in the Army Air Forces and one in the Scots Guards, British Army.

In December of that year, the Club issued a pamphlet listing the sixty-one employees who had served in the war, and hosted a testimonial dinner honoring those members who had served in the war. A number of high-ranking officers attended.

Frederick Walker Castle
USMA, 1930

Frederick Walker Castle joined The University Club in 1941. The following year, he returned to active duty with the army and became an aviator. On Christmas Eve 1944, Brigadier General Castle was piloting a Flying Fortress on a raid over Germany when the failure of one engine caused his aircraft to fall behind the formation. Not wanting to dump his bomb load (which would have improved his maneuverability) for fear of hitting friendly troops, he continued on course. After repeated attacks by enemy fighters, his aircraft was seriously damaged and on fire. He ordered his crew to bail out while remaining at the controls of the stricken aircraft. Before he could escape, the fuel tanks exploded and the plane plunged to earth, taking Castle to his death. In 1946, he was posthumously awarded the Medal of Honor, the sole Club member to receive this distinction.

Winston Churchill

1946

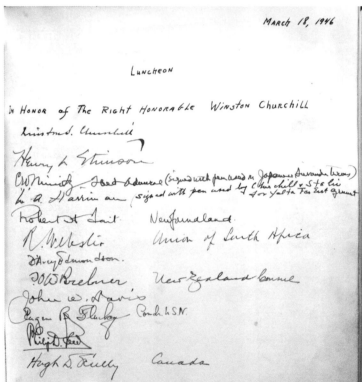

Prior to the luncheon on March 18, 1946, at which Winston S. Churchill spoke, he and other distinguished guests gathered in the Library Atrium for a photograph (above, left). From left to right: Fleet Admiral Chester W. Nimitz, Club president Earle S. Thompson, Churchill, John W. Davis, Henry L. Stimson, former Club president H. Hobart Porter, former Assistant Secretary of War John J. McCloy, Club vice president Edwin S.S. Sunderland, and future Secretary of State John Foster Dulles.

In the Club's guest book for that day, the signature of Winston S. Churchill comes first (above, right). Underneath is that of Henry L. Stimson, a Club member who was Secretary of War from 1940 to 1945. Next comes the signature of Fleet Admiral Chester W. Nimitz, who commanded the U.S. Pacific Fleet during the war. The admiral used the same pen he had used at the Japanese surrender ceremony on board the USS *Missouri* in 1945.

Then we see the signature of W. Averell Harriman, the U.S. ambassador to Great Britain, who had also been the ambassador to the Soviet Union from 1943 to 1946. He would be governor of New York from 1955 to 1958. Not to be outdone by the admiral, Harriman used the pen once used by Churchill and Josef Stalin to sign the Yalta agreement.

A little further down the page, there is the signature of Club member John W. Davis, a prominent lawyer who was one of the founders of the firm known today as Davis, Polk & Wardwell. Davis was the Democratic candidate for president in 1924, but lost to Calvin Coolidge in the general election.

Honoring Veterans

1946

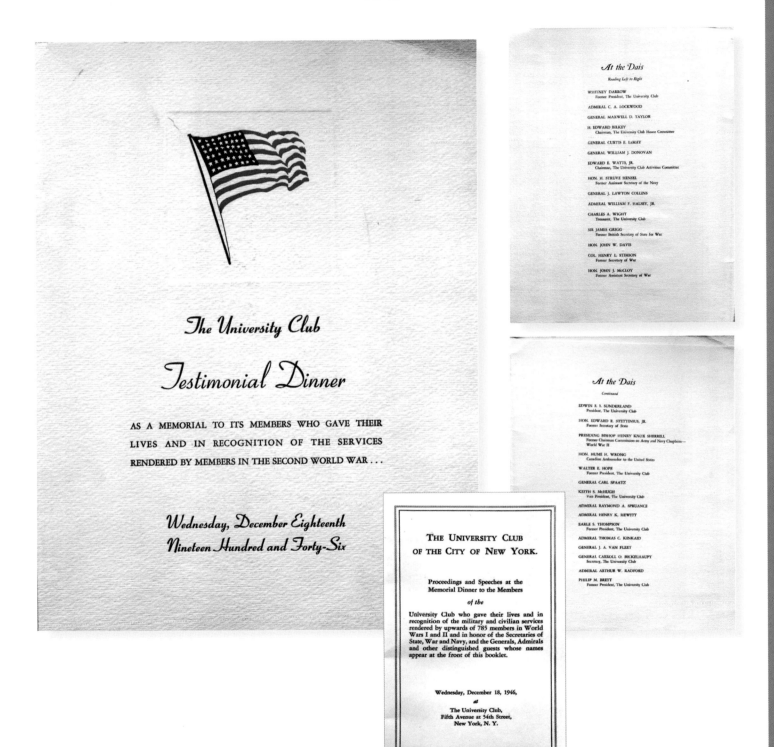

The program for the dinner honoring the eight Club members who were killed in action during the war, and the 700 members who served in both military and civilian capacities

Governor-General of Canada

1947

The University Club Dinner in Honor of
His Excellency, The Governor-General of Canada
Field Marshal Viscount Alexander of Tunis
Monday, February 10th 1947

In 1947, the Club hosted a dinner in honor of the Governor-General of Canada, Field Marshall Viscount Alexander of Tunis. Alexander had had a prominent role in World War II in the Mediterranean theatre. He is standing in the center of the group, wearing a sash.

Metropolitan Opera

1956

The University Club

requests the pleasure of your company

at a

Gala Dinner

in honor of

The Conductors

of the

Metropolitan Opera Association

to be held at

The Club House

on

Tuesday evening, February twenty-eighth

Nineteen hundred and fifty-six

at seven-thirty o'clock

R.S.V.P.   Formal
Enclosed Card   White tie if convenient

Hosting an evening event featuring members of the Metropolitan Opera was a custom for many years.

Mayors of New York City

Luncheon   Mar. 19, 1938
The guest of the Club will be
Hon. Fiorello H. La Guardia
Mayor of the City of New York
Who will speak on   "The City Administration"

Luncheon   April 2, 1938
The speaker will be our fellow member,
Mr. John Foster Dulles

THE UNIVERSITY CLUB OF NEW YORK

requests the pleasure

of your company

at a dinner in honor of

THE MAYOR OF NEW YORK
AND MRS. LINDSAY

on Tuesday

December Tenth

nineteen hundred and sixty-eight

R. S. V. P.
Enclosed Card

THE UNIVERSITY CLUB OF NEW YORK

requests the pleasure

of your company

at a dinner in honor of the

MAYOR OF NEW YORK
AND MRS. BEAME

on Thursday evening,

March Seventh

Nineteen hundred and seventy-four

R. S. V. P.
Enclosed Card

The Guest of Honor and Speaker at the Luncheon on

Saturday, February 27th at 1:15 P. M.

will be

THE HONORABLE ROBERT F. WAGNER

who will speak on

THE JOB OF BEING THE MAYOR

Reception at 12:30 P.M.   CLOYD LAPORTE
Saturday Luncheon Committee   Chairman

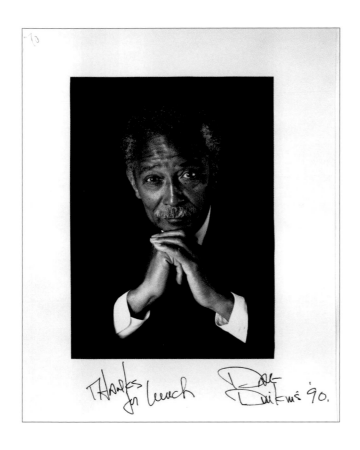

A number of mayors of the City of New York have come to the Club to speak, at either a luncheon or a dinner. The autographed invitations in the Club's archives are shown here. For the more recent mayors, we have photographs that were provided to the Club. Mayor Ed Koch came in 1989, Mayor David Dinkins in 1990, and Rudolph Giuliani came twice: in 1988, when he was the U.S. Attorney for the Southern District of New York, and in 1995 as mayor.

Creative Arts Dinner

1959

The University Club

ANNOUNCES A

Creative Arts Dinner

in recognition of the significance of

LINCOLN CENTER

and of the creative leadership in the organization
and planning of the Center by our fellow member

John D. Rockefeller, 3rd

Wednesday, January 7th, 1959

President's Reception, seven o'clock, Main Lounge
Dinner, seven forty-five o'clock

Black Tie   Ladies may be invited

DAIS

When Lincoln Center for the Performing Arts was in the planning stages,
Club member John D. Rockefeller, 3rd, the first chairman of the board of
the new institution, spoke at the Club. Below his signature in the guest
book is that of Eli Whitney Debevoise, president of the Club from 1957
to 1960.

Luncheon Speakers

The Guest of Honor and Speaker at the Luncheon on
Saturday, February 24th at 1:15 P.M.
will be
THE HONORABLE BARRY GOLDWATER
United States Senator from Arizona
who will speak on
PROBLEMS, POLICIES AND THE FUTURE
Reception at 12:30 P.M.   CLOYD LAPORTE
Saturday Luncheon Committee   Chairman

The Guest of Honor and Speaker at the Luncheon on
Saturday, February 18, 1956 at 1:15 P. M.
will be
HIS EXCELLENCY MAURICE COUVE de MURVILLE
French Ambassador to the United States
who will speak on
"FRANCO - AMERICAN RELATIONS"
Saturday Luncheon Committee   PAULUS P. POWELL
Chairman

The Guest of Honor and Speaker at the Luncheon on
Saturday, December 3rd, at 1:15 P.M.
will be
McGeorge Bundy
President, The Ford Foundation
Formerly Dean of the Faculty of Arts and Sciences Harvard University
and Special Assistant to the President for National Security
who will speak on
"TELEVISION, SATELLITES AND THE PUBLIC INTEREST"
Reception at 12:30 P.M.
Saturday Luncheon Committee   Chairman
ROSS REID

The Guest of Honor and Speaker at the Luncheon on
Saturday, February 24th at 1:15 P.M.
will be
William McChesney Martin, Jr.
Chairman, Board of Governors of the Federal Reserve System
who will speak on
"OBSERVATIONS"
Reception at 12:30 P.M.
Saturday Luncheon Committee   Chairman
RAYMOND C. JOHNSON

The Guest of Honor and Speaker at the Luncheon on
Saturday, December 17th, at 1:15 P.M.
will be
Theodore C. Sorensen, Esq.
Formerly Special Counsel to the President of the United States
and Author of "Kennedy"
who will speak on
"PRINCES AND POTENTATES, AS I HAVE KNOWN THEM"
Reception at 12:30 P.M.
Saturday Luncheon Committee   Chairman
ROSS REID

A group of luncheon speakers from the 1950s and '60s. Maurice Couve de Murville would later be foreign minister of France.

Lord and Lady Snow

1968

THE UNIVERSITY CLUB OF NEW YORK

requests the pleasure

of your company

at a dinner in honor of

LORD SNOW

AND LADY SNOW

on Thursday

October Thirty-first

nineteen hundred and sixty-eight

R. S. V. P.

Enclosed Card

This invitation was the cause of some confusion. Not being aware that the British author C.P. Snow had been raised to the peerage in 1964, and was thereafter formally known as Lord Snow, many members wondered who was coming to the Club. A letter was sent to the membership clarifying that Lord Snow was indeed C.P. Snow, the author of a dozen books, including *Strangers and Brothers*, *The Masters* and *Corridors of Power*. Over a hundred people wound up attending the dinner.

George H.W. Bush

1976

George H.W. Bush, Director, CIA, Langley, Virginia,
March 2, 1976. Photograph by Richard Avedon

THE UNIVERSITY CLUB OF NEW YORK

requests the pleasure

of your company

at a dinner for

THE HONORABLE GEORGE H. W. BUSH
Director
Central Intelligence Agency

on Tuesday

October Fifth

Nineteen hundred and seventy-six

R.S.V.P.
Enclosed Card

William Simon and Griffin Bell

THE UNIVERSITY CLUB OF NEW YORK

requests the pleasure

of your company

at a dinner for

THE HONORABLE WILLIAM E. SIMON

Secretary of the Treasury

on Tuesday

March Thirtieth

Nineteen hundred and seventy-six

R.S.V.P.

Enclosed Card

THE UNIVERSITY CLUB OF NEW YORK

requests the pleasure

of your company

at a dinner for

THE HONORABLE GRIFFIN B. BELL

Attorney General of the United States

on Wednesday

December Fourteenth

Nineteen hundred and seventy-seven

R.S.V.P.

Enclosed Card

Nelson Rockefeller

THE UNIVERSITY CLUB OF NEW YORK

requests the pleasure

of your company

at a dinner with

NELSON A. ROCKEFELLER

Art Collector

on Wednesday

November Fifteenth

Nineteen hundred and seventy-eight

R.S.V.P.

Enclosed Card

Nelson A. Rockefeller, governor of New York from 1959 to 1973 and vice president of the United States from 1974 to 1977, was a member of the Club from 1930 to 1969.

Bridge

1948 – 1949

The University Club

Bridge Season
1948-1949

❦

Card Committee
FRANK W. CHAMBERS
J. RENTON HANEY
WALTER P. LANTZ
W. BARRETT BROWN
Chairman

WALTER F. BAYLIS CUP

This cup will be awarded to the season's champion, who will be the player having the highest average for any 5 of the 8 tournaments. In order to encourage members to play with different partners, no more than 2 scores with the same partner may be included in the season's average.

❦

Member and Guest Tournament
January 26, 1949

❦

College Team of Four Championship for the Ellsworth Eliot, Jr. cup donated by Dr. Seth M. Milliken.

Qualifying Round   March 23, 1949
Finals   March 30

Any four members holding degrees from the same college may enter as a team.

❦

Mixed Pair Tournament - May 18, 1949

Cocktails · · · ·	6:30 P.M.
Dinner · · · · ·	7:00 P.M.
Play Starts · · ·	8:15 P.M.
Last Boards · · ·	11:00 P.M.

RUBBER BRIDGE

Every afternoon 4:00 P.M. to 7:30 P.M.
Wednesday evenings Bridge nights

CLUB DUPLICATE TOURNAMENTS

Club Duplicate Tournaments will be held on
Wednesday evenings. The following time
schedule will apply to each tournament during the season except the mixed pair tournament at the end.

Dinner · · · · ·	7:00 P.M.
Play Starts · · · ·	8:15 P.M.
Last Boards · · ·	11:00 P.M.

Penalties will be imposed on members who are
late when play begins. No new set of boards
will be put in play after 11:00 P.M.

October 27, 1948	February 9, 1949
November 10	March 9
December 1	April 13
January 12, 1949	May 11

INTER-CLUB CONTRACT LEAGUE

1948 -- 1949
SEASON

October 19, 1948 — Opening dinner and pair
game for all.
Union League Club

INTER-CLUB CHAMPIONSHIP

November 16	·	·	University Club
December 7 ·	·	·	Manhattan Club
January 6, 1949 (Thurs.)			Whist Club
April 5	·	·	Union Club

April 19   Individual Championship—
Whist Club — Among leading
players, one from each team.

May 3   Final dinner and pair game for all.
New York Athletic Club.

All games are on Tuesday evenings, except
Thursday, January 6, 1949 (dress informal).
Each is preceded by assembly of participants
at 6:30 sharp. Dinner at 7:00 P.M. sharp!

Dinner Dance

1950s

Two invitations for annual dinner dances

Events

MONUMENTS
OF MANHATTAN

*AN EXHIBITION OF GREAT BUILDINGS
IN NEW YORK CITY, 1800–1918*

JANUARY 1ST TO MARCH 15TH, 1955

'*Objets inanimés, avez-vous donc une âme
Qui s'attache à notre âme et la force d'aimer?*'
LAMARTINE

THE UNIVERSITY CLUB

UNDER THE SPONSORSHIP OF THE UNIVERSITY
CLUB AND THE MUNICIPAL ART SOCIETY
NEW YORK CITY

CLUB ACTIVITIES COMMITTEE • THE UNIVERSITY CLUB, 1 WEST 54th ST.

THIRTEENTH ANNUAL SAFARI
TO THE BRONX ZOO

Safari Number Thirteen Is Getting Set
To Wander Through The Zoo!
So far We've Always Had Much Fun.
Wouldn't You Like To Too?

May 7th is the day for our Thirteenth Safari to the Zoo. We had a simply wonderful time last year and the children too young for Safari Twelve will just love Safari Thirteen. Those of you who had to borrow children can again build up credit standing.

THE DATE: Saturday, May 7, 1955.
THE TIME: 1:30 P.M.
THE PLACE: Zoobar Restaurant, opposite the Elephant House.

THE UNIVERSITY CLUB SPECIAL TRACTOR TRAIN will meet you at the South Gate if you come by subway, and carry you to the Zoobar. Look for the UNIVERSITY CLUB sign inside the gate.

BY SUBWAY, you can reach the Park in about 50 minutes from downtown, 35 minutes from midtown Manhattan.

East Side Subway (I.R.T.): Take a northbound 241 St. - White Plains Road Express (or an East 180 St. Express) to 177th Street. Walk north to Zoo.

West Side Subway (I.R.T.): Just take a northbound East 180 St. Express to 177th Street. Walk north to Zoo.

BRING THE WHOLE FAMILY: This is not a *stag* party. The entire family is invited. Plenty of room. Plenty to see. Plenty of fun.

THE PRICE: Luncheon $2.00 (including gratuities). After Luncheon the Zoo is ours.

SATURDAY LUNCHEON COMMITTEE

THE UNIVERSITY CLUB.
SATURDAY LUNCHEON COMMITTEE.

I shall attend the Thirteenth Annual Safari to the Bronx Zoo.

I shall bring .... guests.

....
Signature.

(Charge $2.00 per person (including gratuities). Your committee will appreciate a prompt reply.)

Above: Announcement of an exhibit at the Club
Right: Invitation to Bronx Zoo outing, then an annual event

Dinner Honoring Harold Helm
Lunch Honoring Prime Minister of Australia

1953 – 1955

When Harold Helm stepped down as president of the Club in 1953, the Council honored him at a dinner.

Luncheon
in honor of
The Right Honorable John G. Menzies
Prime Minister of Australia
given by
The Mayor of the City of New York

Menu

Coupe of Fresh Fruit

Burgundy,
Beaujolais

Roast Prime Ribs of Beef
Pan Gravy
Chateau Potatoes
Garden String Beans au Gratin

Pineapple Sherbet
Petits Fours

Demi Tasse

University Club   March 7, 1955

Menu for a (rare) official luncheon held at the Club

Gala Dinner

1960

The President and The Council
of
The University Club
request the pleasure of the company of

at a

Gala Dinner
arranged by
The Musical Affairs Committee
in honor of
Mr. Lauder Greenway, Chairman of the Board
and
Mr. Anthony A. Bliss, President
of the
Metropolitan Opera Association
on
Tuesday evening, March fifteenth
Nineteen hundred and sixty
at seven-thirty o'clock

R. S. V. P.   Formal Dress
The Musical Affairs Committee   (White tie preferred)
The University Club
1 West 54th Street
New York 19

A dinner honoring members of the Metropolitan Opera Association

Dinners

1961 – 1963

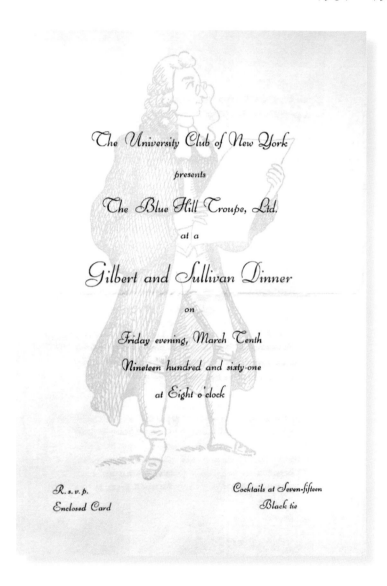

Left: The Blue Hill Troupe were regular guests at the Club, as they are to the present day. **Right:** With the destruction of Pennsylvania Station imminent, the Club hosted this dinner to address the topic of historic preservation.

Centennial Dinners

1965

The Officers and The Council of

THE UNIVERSITY CLUB

request the pleasure of your company

at a

CENTENNIAL DINNER

to be held at

THE UNIVERSITY CLUB

on Thursday, February fourth

and Wednesday, February seventeenth

nineteen hundred and sixty-five

at six forty-five o'clock

R. S. V. P. *(Card enclosed)* · *Black or White Tie*

The centennial was celebrated with various events in 1965.

In celebration of our

CENTENNIAL YEAR

*The Officers and The Council
cordially invite you to be a guest of*

THE UNIVERSITY CLUB

at a

RECEPTION AND BUFFET DINNER

*to be held on Tuesday, January Twelfth
nineteen hundred and sixty-five
from five-thirty to nine o'clock*

R. S. V. P. *(card enclosed)*

INFORMAL

THE UNIVERSITY CLUB

CENTENNIAL DINNER

1865-1965

February fourth, nineteen hundred and sixty-five

Leeward Island Cruise

1968

Raymond & Whitcomb Company
INVITES THE MEMBERS OF
The University Club

TO VISIT

THE LEEWARD & WINDWARD ISLANDS of the West Indies

February 17 - March 2
1968

YOU ARE INVITED to join fellow Club members* on the 4500-ton cruising yacht M.T.S. Argonaut during the festive Carnival period preceding Lent for a special voyage through unspoiled islands of natural beauty and interest, many inaccessable to large cruise ships and scheduled airlines.

Fly by scheduled Pan American Jet Clipper between New York and San Juan, where you board your ship. Sail during the night on a fourteen day voyage, arriving each morning in a different island (eliminating bothersome packing and unpacking).

New York to New York rates are from $695 to $1070 per person, double, with rooms alone at higher rates. Special rates will be quoted for flights from other cities and other than those specified in the itinerary. Arrangements for extensions prior to or after the return to San Juan can be arranged.

Arrangements for the program have been made by Raymond & Whitcomb Co. Requests for additional information and reservations should be directed to that agency. Raymond & Whitcomb can be reached by phone through the Club (by asking for "travel"), directly at PLaza 9-3960, or at their office, 400 Madison Avenue, New York, New York 10017.

This program is arranged solely as an accommodation for members of the Club. Neither The University Club nor its officers, employees or members accepts any responsibility or liability in connection with this trip.

*Also invited are family and friends travelling with members. No public solicitation is contemplated. Reservation requests will be accepted in the order they are received.

THE LEEWARD & WINDWARD ISLANDS of the West Indies 1968

OUTLINE ITINERARY

Leave New York on Saturday morning, February 17th, by non-stop jet flight to Puerto Rico. Transfer on arrival to the charming El Convento Hotel in Old San Juan for an informal reception, buffet, and visit to nearby historic buildings, narrow streets and colorful markets recalling its Spanish heritage. Dinner will be served on board. The Argonaut sails at 10:00 P.M. on the following itinerary, with the last column indicating the approximate hours at each port of call:

February	Day	Port	Arrival	Stay (in hours)
18	Sun.	St. Croix	Early morning	16
19	Mon.	Nevis	Early morning	4
		St. Kitts	Midday	6
20	Tues.	Iles des Saintes	Early morning	3
		Dominica	Mid-afternoon	6
21	Wed.	St. Lucia	Early morning	15
22	Thurs.	Bequia	Early morning	4
		St. Vincent	Midday	17
23	Fri.	Carriacou	Early morning	3
		Grenada	Mid-afternoon	35.5
24	Sat.	In Grenada		
25	Sun.	Tobago	Early morning	13
26	Mon.	Trinidad	Pre-dawn	13
27	Tues.	Martinique	Mid-morning	14
28	Wed.	Antigua	Midday	10
29	Thurs.	Virgin Gorda	Mid-morning	3
		St. Thomas	Mid-afternoon	34.5
March				
1	Fri.	In St. Thomas		

The voyage will terminate in San Juan at 8:00 A.M. on Saturday, March 2. Transfer with luggage to the airport, departing later that day by jet flight.

A brochure describing a trip offered to members

Facilities Brochure

1967

Club facilities list for the 1960s

DINING ROOMS

MAIN DINING ROOM — 7th Floor
Breakfast: 7 A.M. to 11 A.M.
Luncheon: 12 Noon to 2:30 P.M.
Dinner: 6 P.M. to 9 P.M.

Open Monday through Saturday. Closed for Dinner on Friday and Breakfast, Luncheon and Dinner on Saturday during Summer.

GRILL ROOM — 2nd Floor
Luncheon: 12 Noon to 2:30 P.M.
Sunday Brunch: 8 A.M. to 1 P.M.
Open for Breakfast, Luncheon and Dinner on Saturday (Modified Menu) during Summer

Open Monday through Friday.

LADIES' DINING ROOM AND COCKTAIL LOUNGE
Main Floor
Luncheon: 12 Noon to 2:30 P.M.
Dinner: 6 P.M. to 9 P.M.
Members must be accompanied by a Lady

Open Monday through Saturday. Closed on Saturday during Summer.

PRIVATE DINING ROOMS
College Hall, Oak Room — Main Floor
Room 6 — 2nd Floor
Council, Breakfast Rooms — 7th Floor
Rooms A, B, C — 7th Floor
Rooms 1, 2, 3, 4 and 5 — 9th Floor
Only Male Guests May Be Invited
To The Private Dining Rooms

Available to members for meetings and private parties. For Information Call Maitre d'Hotel.

TAP ROOM — 2nd Floor
Open Monday through Saturday: 11 A.M. to 1 A.M.
Open Sunday: 1 P.M. to 9 P.M.
Sandwiches Available on Sundays After 1 P.M.

Closes at 9 P.M. on Saturday during Summer.

OYSTER BAR — 2nd Floor
12 Noon to 2 P.M.
5:30 P.M. to 7 P.M.

Open Monday through Friday in Season Only.

BEDROOMS
94 Single Bedrooms, 10 Suites. Available on Transient or Annual Basis
Pressing, Cleaning, Laundry.
Television Rental, Storage Lockers.
Check Out Time — 3 P.M. — Late Departing Guests are Requested to Check Luggage in Check Room on Main Floor.

Call Valet.

FRONT DESK — Main Floor
Bedroom Reservations
Applications for Guest Privileges
Check Cashing
Telegrams
Theatre Tickets
Tobacco Products
Car Rental
Mail, Messages

See Clerk on Duty.

BATH DEPARTMENT — Basement Floor
Swimming Pool
Licensed Masseurs
Hot and Steam Rooms
Ultra-violet and Infra-red Lamps
Exercise Room

Open Monday through Friday 11 A.M. to 7:30 P.M. Open Saturday 11 A.M. to 7:00 P.M. Closed on Saturdays during Summer.

BILLIARD ROOM — 5th Floor

Attendant on duty from 2:30 P.M., Monday through Saturday.

CARD ROOM — 4th Floor

Attendant on duty from 4:30 P.M., Monday through Friday.

LIBRARY, MAGAZINE, CHESS ROOMS — 4th Floor

Two librarians are on duty Monday through Saturday 9:30 A.M. to 5 P.M. for readers' advisory services.

SQUASH COURTS — 10th Floor
7 Singles Courts
1 Doubles Court

Call Squash Pro for Matches, Lessons, Equipment, Lockers.

BARBER SHOP — 2nd Floor

Open Monday through Saturday 8 A.M. to 6 P.M. Closed on Saturdays during Summer. Manicurist services are available from Monday through Friday 10 A.M. to 4:30 P.M.

Events

1971 – 1973

THE UNIVERSITY CLUB OF NEW YORK

requests the pleasure of your company at a

"Joy of Wine"

Dinner on Wednesday, October thirty-first

Nineteen hundred and seventy-three

with

H. GREGORY THOMAS

R.S.V.P.
Card Enclosed

THE UNIVERSITY CLUB
NEW YORK

New Year's Day Reception

FOR MEMBERS ONLY

All members are invited to attend the traditional Annual Egg Nog Party which will be held in College Hall on Friday, January 1, 1971 from 12 noon to 2 P.M.

A buffet luncheon will be served at which members will have the opportunity to exchange season's greetings.

ANNUAL EVENTS COMMITTEE

THE HOUSE COMMITTEE

THE UNIVERSITY CLUB
NEW YORK

The Musical Affairs Committee is pleased to announce a Musicale on Sunday afternoon, January 23, 1972, featuring

CAROL LONGONE

assisted by five attractive young artists

•

in an Operalogue production in costume of

MADAME BUTTERFLY

Program in the Main Lounge at 4:15 promptly. Cocktails, coffee and tea in College Hall afterwards. Orchestra, under Leo Pleskow, in the Main Lounge from 3:45 to 4:15 and in College Hall during the refreshment period.

Both men and women guests may be invited. Charge $7.50 per person, plus tax, including refreshments. Please mail the attached card promptly.

The University Club

requests the pleasure of your company

at a

Birthday Dinner Dance

in honor of George Washington

on

Friday Evening, February 23, 1973

at nine o'clock

Complimentary Cocktails in the Main Lounge

at eight o'clock

Bill Halfacre's Orchestra

R.S.V.P.   *$15 Per Person*

Enclosed Card   *Black Tie*

THE UNIVERSITY CLUB
NEW YORK

TO ALL MEMBERS

Many New York clubs and others throughout the country are increasing dues by an amount equal to all or part of the 20% Federal Excise Tax on Club Dues previously in effect but which has been repealed effective January 1, 1966.

We are pleased to annouce that a review of the current financial position of The University Club indicates there is no present need or justification for increasing our dues and you will, therefore, receive the entire benefit of the elimination of this Federal Tax.

Harold A. Rousselot
Treasurer

12/1/65

UNIVERSITY CLUB WEEK

SKIING SWISS POWDER

$330

per person plus $33 covering
taxes and service charges

including

TRANSPORTATION - ACCOMMODATIONS - MEALS

(other passengers on your scheduled KLM flights will be paying the low-season economy fare of $507 for air transportation alone)

SATURDAY, MARCH 20 to SUNDAY, MARCH 28
1971

In 1971, the Club offered members a week of skiing in Switzerland.

Dissolution of Educational Foundation

1971

**EDUCATIONAL FOUNDATION
OF THE UNIVERSITY CLUB, INC.
New York**

May 14, 1971

TO OUR FELLOW MEMBERS OF THE UNIVERSITY CLUB:

As the Members and Directors of the Educational Foundation of The University Club, Inc., we wish to advise you, in this our final report, of the decision to dissolve the Foundation, and to distribute its assets as a gift to the New York Public Library.

Following the passage of the Tax Reform Act of 1969, the Directors of the Foundation gave serious study and consideration to the question of whether the Foundation should undergo dissolution or continue under the Act. Many reasons prompted our decision to dissolve, but among the more compelling were the following: the onerous impact of the Tax Reform Act on small "private foundations" such as the Educational Foundation, including an investment income tax, numerous reports, and an expected increase in accounting fees; the limited income of the Foundation available for grants (well under $8,000 per year, including annual contributions from members of the Club); and the fact that the Foundation largely served as a channel for contributions from a relatively few members of the Club to certain organizations in education, music, and the arts, to which organizations these Club members henceforth can make, if they wish, tax deductible contributions without recourse to the Foundation.

The plan for dissolving the Foundation through the distribution of its assets of about $80,000 to the New York Public Library has been concurred in by the Council of the Club and approved by the appropriate New York State judicial and administrative agencies. It is expected that the Foundation will cease to exist within the next ninety days.

In making the gift of the Foundation's assets to the New York Public Library, the Directors have specified and the Library has agreed to the following conditions: (a) that the principal of the assets received from the Foundation by the New York Public Library, including the $25,000 Harry L. Parr Fund, forever remain intact, in a fund to be designated by the Public Library as "The University Club Book Purchase Fund"; (b) that the Public Library separately subdesignate $25,000 of the total University Club Book Purchase Fund as the "Harry L. Parr Fund"; (c) that the income from The University Club Book Purchase Fund, including the income from the Harry L. Parr Fund, be spent for the purchase of books, with the Public Library giving preference to books published by university presses; and (d) that a book plate be inserted in each such book acknowledging the gift of The University Club Book Purchase Fund.

The New York Public Library aids students and faculties from universities and colleges throughout the country by providing unique research facilities and scholarly resources. Also, university press organizations will be strengthened by having the Library give preference to purchasing their publications. Consequently, and because two of the principal purposes for which the Foundation was formed were (a) to aid education and universities, and (b) to aid libraries, we believe that giving our assets to the New York Public Library is a particularly appropriate disposition of them, and one which will meet with the approval of all members of the Club.

In closing this report, we wish to remind any member of The University Club who may have made the Educational Foundation a beneficiary in his will to make appropriate changes. In so doing, perhaps consideration could be given to a suggestion that has been advanced that provision be made in favor of the Club itself.*

Respectfully submitted,

Julian B. Beaty, Jr.	Robert N. Kreidler	Albert G. Redpath
R. Manning Brown	George J. Leness	Harold A. Rousselot
A. Fairfield Dana	George B. Munroe	Charles E. Saltzman
Eli Whitney Debevoise	James Quigg Newton	Julian Street, Jr.
Joseph A. Grazier	LeRoy A. Petersen	Edward Townsend

Members and Directors

---

*In this regard, we should call to your attention the fact that, although The University Club is a tax-exempt and non-profit organization, it is not a charitable organization as defined by the Internal Revenue Code, and thus bequests to it are not deductible for estate tax purposes. Despite this fact, however, the Club has received many bequests from members over the years, either for the general purposes of the Club or, particularly, for the Club's Library.

Family Night

Various Dates

The University Club

is pleased to announce its

FIRST ANNUAL
FAMILY NIGHT DINNER

THURSDAY, DECEMBER 28, 1972

Featuring

YOUR FATHER'S
MUSTACHE

World famous banjo band, fresh from appearances with the Boston Pops, the Mike Douglas Show, and schools and colleges everywhere.

Join in an old fashioned sing-a-long with free straw hats for everyone, mustaches for all the gentlemen.

Bring Your Family - Or Let Them Bring You !

If necessary, borrow a family. All ages welcome. Wives, daughters, grandparents, sons, nephews, nieces, cousins, school chums. Invite them all for an evening of stupendous entertainment, great food and holiday festivity.

RECEPTION STARTS AT 6 P.M.

FREE REFRESHMENTS !

Reservations will be accepted in order of receipt. Families wishing to sit together should inform Mr. Paul Wood at the Club Office — CIrcle 7-2100. Members are urged to return the enclosed reservation card immediately. Cancellations cannot be credited after 10 A.M. December 27th.

RECEPTION 6 P.M. MAIN LOUNGE   DRESS INFORMAL

PRE-DINNER REFRESHMENTS AND DINNER $7.50 (plus tax) per person

THE UNIVERSITY CLUB
1 West 54th Street, New York, N. Y. 10019

ANNUAL EVENTS COMMITTEE
RICHARD L. BRECKER, *Chairman*

BRUCE ANGUS   DON DURGIN
ALAN S. McDOWELL   LANNY ROSS

The University Club

*invites you and your family
to participate in its*

EIGHTH ANNUAL FAMILY NIGHT

THURSDAY, DECEMBER 27, 1979

During the Reception and Dinner

THE DOWNTOWN BLUE BLOWERS
Will Entertain With
DIXIELAND JAZZ

After Dinner

MICHAEL E. BERLANT, MAGICIAN

Will entertain both young and old with his

CARNIVAL OF MAGIC

Featuring mystifying magic, balloons,
and lively carnival music

The Annual Family Night falls between the joyful Christmas and festive New Year's holidays and combines the warmth and excitement of both. In its eighth consecutive year, this event promises to maintain the tradition of previous years as a most popular and happy event for our members and their families and friends. Bring your wife and children, friends and their families, to share in the fun and conviviality.

Reservations will be accepted in order of receipt. Due to the anticipated heavy holiday mail, members should call Mr. Normand Bordeleau at the Club Office, 572-3403 for reservations and seating. Members are also urged to return the enclosed reservation card immediately. Cancellations cannot be credited after 10 A.M., December 26th.

REFRESHMENTS 6 P.M. MAIN LOUNGE   DRESS INFORMAL
PRE-DINNER REFRESHMENTS AND DINNER $13 (plus tax) per person

THE UNIVERSITY CLUB
1 West 54th Street, New York, N.Y. 10019

ANNUAL EVENTS COMMITTEE
PAUL FENWICK, Chairman

GERALD F. ABBOTT   MALCOLM ANDRESEN
JEROME P. CORTELLESI   JOSE L. DeCUBAS
WILLIAM H. HAGENDORN   ALLEN B. HOLETT
SAMUEL J. MURRAY   EUGENE R. SULLIVAN

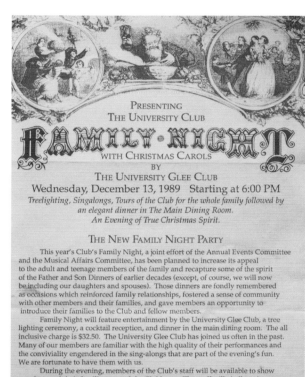

PRESENTING
THE UNIVERSITY CLUB

FAMILY·NIGHT
WITH CHRISTMAS CAROLS
BY
THE UNIVERSITY GLEE CLUB
Wednesday, December 13, 1989   Starting at 6:00 PM
*Treelighting, Singalongs, Tours of the Club for the whole family followed by
an elegant dinner in The Main Dining Room.
An Evening of True Christmas Spirit.*

THE NEW FAMILY NIGHT PARTY

This year's Club's Family Night, a joint effort of the Annual Events Committee and the Musical Affairs Committee, has been planned to increase its appeal to the adult and teenage members of the family and recapture some of the spirit of the Father and Son Dinners of earlier decades (except, of course, we will now be including our daughters and spouses). Those dinners are fondly remembered as occasions which reinforced family relationships, fostered a sense of community with other members and their families, and gave members an opportunity to introduce their families to the Club and fellow members.

Family Night will feature entertainment by the University Glee Club, a tree lighting ceremony, a cocktail reception, and dinner in the main dining room. The all inclusive charge is $32.50. The University Glee Club has joined us often in the past. Many of our members are familiar with the high quality of their performances and the conviviality engendered in the sing-alongs that are part of the evening's fun. We are fortunate to have them with us.

During the evening, members of the Club's staff will be available to show members and their families around the Clubhouse. The staff will gladly point out, with some justifiable pride, the new and refurbished facilities which have been completed to date and explain some of the work still on progress.

*Please send your reservation card early,
or simply phone the Manager's Office at 572-3403/4.*

Subscription $32.50
(Children 8 years and older are welcome)   (OVER)

In 1972, the father and son and father and daughter dinners were consolidated into Family Night, which continues to this day.

Museum Directors Dinner and Talk

1973

THE UNIVERSITY CLUB OF NEW YORK

requests the pleasure of your company

at a dinner in honor of

DUNCAN CAMERON
DIRECTOR OF THE BROOKLYN MUSEUM

and

RICHARD E. OLDENBURG
DIRECTOR OF THE MUSEUM OF MODERN ART

on Thursday, February eighth

Nineteen hundred and seventy-three

R.S.V.P.
Card enclosed

Another event featuring people prominent in the cultural life of the city

Speaker Events

Various Dates

The Guest of Honor and Speaker at the Luncheon on Saturday, February 22nd, at 1:15 P.M. will be

GENERAL GEORGE S. BROWN, U.S.A.F.
Chairman of the Joint Chiefs of Staff

who will speak on

"NATIONAL DEFENSE"

General Brown was graduated from the U.S. Military Academy in 1941. He received his pilot wings at Kelly Field, Texas in 1942.

After a highly impressive war record, General Brown held increasingly important military positions. He became Chief of Staff of the United States Air Force on August 1, 1973 and served until his appointment as Chairman of the Joint Chiefs of Staff effective July 1, 1974.

General Brown holds an extensive list of decorations and service awards.

LADIES ARE INVITED

Reception 12:30 P.M.
Dinner and Lecture Committee

Luncheon 1:15 P.M.
Edward R. Finch, Jr., Chairman

The Guest of Honor and Speaker at the Luncheon on

Saturday, January 14th, at 1:15 P.M.

will be

General Lucius D. Clay
U.S. Army, Retired; Senior Partner, Lehman Brothers; Former Commander-in-Chief U.S. Forces in Europe.

Reception at 12:30 P.M.

Saturday Luncheon Committee

Chairman
ROSS REID

The Guest of Honor and Speaker at the Luncheon on Tuesday, April 6, 1976 at 12:00 P.M. will be

THOMAS A. MURPHY
Chairman of the Board and Chief Executive Officer, General Motors Corporation

who will speak on

"UNFINISHED BUSINESS OF AMERICA"

Thomas A. Murphy received his Bachelor of Science Degree in Accounting from the University of Illinois in 1938. He joined GM immediately following graduation.

Mr. Murphy was elected Chairman of the Board of Directors of General Motors and Chief Executive Officer of the Corporation effective December 1, 1974. He is Chairman of GM's Finance Committee and a member of the Executive and Administrative Committees.

LADIES ARE INVITED

Reception 12:00 P.M.
Adjournment before 2:00 P.M.

Luncheon 12:20 P.M.

The Guest of Honor and Speaker at the Luncheon on

Wednesday, November 21st at 12:00 P.M. will be

DR. ALAN GREENSPAN

who will speak on

"ECONOMIC OUTLOOK — THE 80's"

Dr. Greenspan served as Chairman of the President's Council of Economic Advisers under President Ford. Currently he is Adjunct Professor of Economics, Graduate School of Business Administration, NYU, serves as a member of The Council on Foreign Relations and is Chairman and President of Townsend-Greenspan & Co., Inc., an economics consulting firm.

LADIES ARE INVITED

Reception 12:00 P.M.
Adjournment before 2:00 P.M.

Luncheon 12:20 P.M.

The Guest of Honor and Speaker at the Luncheon on Monday, February 1st at 12:00 P.M. will be

GEORGE STEINBRENNER
Owner of the New York Yankees

LADIES ARE INVITED

Reception 12:00 P.M.
Adjournment before 2:00 P.M.

Luncheon 12:20 P.M.

Dinner and Lecture Committee

Max M. Ulrich, Chairman

By the 1970s, some of the luncheon speakers came during the week, rather than on Saturday.

Annual Meetings

1977 and 1984

THE UNIVERSITY CLUB
Annual Meeting and Dinner

Musical Entertainment by the

THE WEST POINT GLEE CLUB

Tuesday, May 10, 1977

5:00 Cocktails in the Atrium — Members Only
5:30 Annual Meeting in the Main Lounge — Members Only
6:15 Reception and Dinner — Members and Guests
After Dinner Concert by The West Point Glee Club

INFORMAL DRESS

Wives and Guests Welcome

R.S.V.P.   Cocktail Reception and Dinner
Enclosed Card $13.50 per person (plus tax)

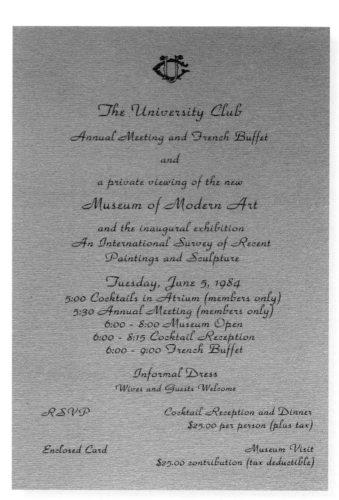

For a number of years, the custom was to provide entertainment on the day of the annual meeting.

First Issue of *The Bulletin* with Cover Art

1978

The Bulletin of the University Club

New York, December 1978

The Hon. John J. McCloy

John McCloy Reminisces

On December 6, the Honorable John J. McCloy will keynote a landmark dinner honoring more than 800 members distinguished by 25 years or more of membership in the Club.

Mr. McCloy, a member of the Club since 1924, has played a varied and prominent role in public life through the Administrations of half a dozen Presidents, serving as Assistant Secretary of War, President of the World Bank, U.S. Military Governor and High Commissioner for Germany, and advisor to President Kennedy. Currently a partner in the law firm of Millbank, Tweed, Hadley and McCloy, he has been chairman of the board of the Chase Manhattan Bank and the Ford Foundation.

A much sought after speaker, Mr. McCloy will share with the honored quarter-century members an evening of "Recollections of an Older Member."

This special event is open to all members of the Club, and younger members are encouraged to attend both in tribute to the senior members, and to take advantage of an excellent opportunity to become acquainted with the fascinating history of the Club over the past half-century, and the many renowned figures who have graced our company with their presence.

An Historical Note On the Coat Tails Of John McCloy

There is another dimension to the pleasure of membership in the University Club, and the enjoyment of its facilities and activities: that of being part of a living tradition and a company of men who, over the past century, have left their mark upon this city and in many cases, this nation and the history of our time.

The Club had an auspicious beginning in 1865. By chance, an early clubhouse had been the home of the grandfather of Winston Churchill.

Since then, the Club's landmark building has known the presence of a fascinating array of historic figures as members and as guests.

Winston Churchill made an important speech at the Club in 1946.

Somerset Maugham worked in the library. So did A.J. Cronin and a good many other literary figures. Lord Halifax, the British Foreign Secretary, drafted speeches there.

The University Club is peopled by history, and we are heirs of a grand tradition.

In future issues of the Club Bulletin, we will present an anecdotal history of the Club and the men who, over the past 113 years, have been part of it.

Annual Christmas Fund

Members will soon receive the annual appeal for the Employees Christmas Fund. Since Club rules prohibit tipping, the fund is the traditional means through which members acknowledge the excellent service by the staff that has come to be a hallmark of the Club.

A number of familiar faces have been with the Club for many years. As always, the fund is distributed with recognition for length of service.

With the spectre of recession around the corner, it is hoped that members will be buoyant and expansive this year in using the fund to thank our employees, anticipating the possibility of being in a foul mood next year.

Events

PLAYBILL

The University Club

BROADWAY MEMORIES

The Musical Affairs Committee
April 11, 1986

THE UNIVERSITY CLUB

cordially invites you to attend

AN EVENING WITH GEORGE FEYER

Monday evening, January 9, 1978

Complimentary cocktails in the
Main Lounge at six-thirty

R.S.V.P. $15.00 Per Person (Plus Tax)
Card Enclosed   Informal Dress

PULI TORO

Puli Toro, mezzo-soprano, is a soloist with the New York City Opera and has appeared regularly with that company during their New York seasons at Lincoln Center, at the Kennedy Center in Washington, and at the Music Center in Los Angeles. The spring of '81 season at City Opera featured her in their revival of Janacek's "The Makropoulous Affair" and "The Cunning Little Vixen".

She has appeared in the "Live from Lincoln Center" series in productions such as "Ballad of Baby Doe" and most recently, had the distinction of being invited to participate in Beverly Sills's Farewell Performance at the New York City Opera.

She scored a great success as Rosina in the "Barber of Seville", at the Teatro Municipal in Caracas; made outstanding contributions in the trouser roles of Cherubino, Siebel and Stephano. Throughout the United States she has been seen in a variety of roles with opera companies of Pittsburgh, Orlando, Toledo, Dayton, as well as in her native Puerto Rico.

In 1974 High Fidelity Magazine included her in their selection of "New Faces". In 1977 she was named "Opera Singer of the Year" by the Institute of Puerto Rico in New York City.

Puli Toro's versatility has found fertile ground in operetta at the New York City Center, as well as in musical comedy and Spanish Zarzuelas. Her extensive repertoire, which includes the standard orchestral pieces for mezzo, has made her a sought after recitalist of art songs and chamber music.

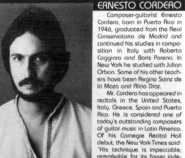

ERNESTO CORDERO

Composer-guitarist Ernesto Cordero, born in Puerto Rico in 1946, graduated from the Real Conservatorio de Madrid and continued his studies in composition in Italy with Roberto Caggiaro and Boris Porena. In New York he studied with Julian Orbon. Some of his other teachers have been Regino Sainz de la Maza and Alirio Diaz.

Mr. Cordero has appeared in recitals in the United States, Italy, Greece, Spain and Puerto Rico. He is considered one of today's outstanding composers of guitar music in Latin America. Of his Carnegie Recital Hall debut, the New York Times said: "His technique is impeccable, remarkable for its finger independence and ability to clarify and articulate the most complex textures. His compositions revealed an interesting creative impulse: they projected a healthy combination of skill, sensitive invention and sound musical effect."

Several of Cordero's works have been published by Spanish Music Center in New York and G. Zanibon, Italian publishing firm internationally represented.

PROGRAM WILL INCLUDE WORKS BY:
HANDEL, CORDERO, LORCA, DEL VADO,
FUENLLANA, PISADOR

**The Backgammon-Chess Committee
of The University Club**

cordially invites our members and their guests to participate in the BENJAMIN FRANKLIN BACKGAMMON EVENING on Tuesday, January 17, 1984.

Starting with informal play at 5:30 p.m., this evening will commemorate the birthday of Benjamin Franklin (b. 1706), "Elder Statesman of the American Revolution" and author of "Poor Richard's' Almanac." Ladies are welcome.

Informal play at 5:30 p.m.; tournament to begin at 7:00 p.m.

Poor Richard Dinner at 8:00 p.m.; tournament conclusion by 10:30 p.m.

Younger Men's Activities Committee

Department of the Treasury

**Internal Revenue
Service Center
North-Atlantic Region**

Date:	In reply refer to:
	JMC 212

Dear Taxpayer:

RE: "... the 1040 Blues"

The Service wishes to bring to your attention the Spring Dinner Dance of the Younger Men's Activities Committee at the University Club, entitled "... the 1040 Blues". The event is scheduled for April 18, 1975. At fifteen dollars a person, you will barely blow your rebate.

You are expected at 7:15 p.m. at which time late filers are invited to review their deductions with our personnel. In keeping with the seriousness of the matter, a "black tie" is preferred.

During pre-dinner consultations, you will be served a Derby drink on us, as part of our extensive rebate program. Appropriate "blues" numbers by Eddie Locke and his "All Stars" will be aud(it)ible.

At 9:00 p.m., after your appointment, you will move into a Kentucky Derby Dinner where a non-deductible wager on the Derby favorites might not enable you to cover your tax liability, but might win you a weekend for two at the Churchill Downs event. Dancing to the Bob Thomas Orchestra will continue until 1:00 a.m. and it's guaranteed that by evening's end you will have gotten over "... the 1040 Blues".

Younger Men's Activities Committee

THE UNIVERSITY CLUB

COCKTAILS — 7:15 PM
DINNER — 9:00 PM

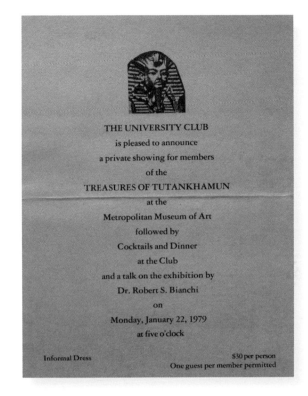

THE UNIVERSITY CLUB

is pleased to announce

a private showing for members

of the

TREASURES OF TUTANKHAMUN

at the

Metropolitan Museum of Art

followed by

Cocktails and Dinner

at the Club

and a talk on the exhibition by

Dr. Robert S. Bianchi

on

Monday, January 22, 1979

at five o'clock

Informal Dress $30 per person
One guest per member permitted

The Younger Men's Activities Committee

cordially invites you to attend

A SHEIK AFFAIR

Club Members Going to Europe

Club members preparing to board their charter flight to Europe, May 5, 1961

Viennese Ball Invitation

1988

Friday, March 11, 1988

The Musical Affairs Committee cordially invites you to come to the Viennese Ball, a white tie event which will recreate the aristocratic elegance of the Imperial Era. We are working closely with the Club's staff in order to arrange a very special evening that will be remembered by you and yours for many years to come.

The services of the acclaimed Orchestra New England have been retained for a full four hour performance of the finest classical waltzes, by members of the Strauss family and by other great composers, including the complete "Emperor" as well as many other favorite melodies.

Cocktails, champagne and a delicious, authentic Austrian dinner (including complimentary wine) will be served to begin the evening; the cotillion follows, and midway through the party, we will serve a full Viennese Table replete with hundreds of pastries, freshly baked for the occasion.

Please reserve your place by calling the Manager's Office at 572-3403/4.

The Viennese Ball

Schedule of Events

6:30 P.M.-7:30 P.M.
Cocktails and Champagne
Main Reading Room

7:30 P.M.-9:00 P.M.
Dinner
College Hall

9:00 P.M.-1:00 A.M.
Ballroom Dancing
Main Dining Room

10:00 P.M.-11:30 P.M.
Viennese Coffee Hour
Council Room

Dress will be White-Tie*
Price: $75.00 plus tax

*Black-tie also acceptable

Kennedy Administration Officials' Letters

THE ATTORNEY GENERAL
WASHINGTON
February 15, 1961

Dear Mr. Magill:

I want to thank you for your kind letter of January 30th and the cordial invitation to use the facilities of the University Club when I am in New York. This courtesy is greatly appreciated.

Sincerely,

Robert F. Kennedy

Mr. Roswell Magill
President
The University Club
One West Fifty-Fourth Street
New York 19, New York

THE WHITE HOUSE
WASHINGTON

February 23, 1961

Dear Mr. Magill:

I wish to thank you and the members of the University Club for offering me the privileges of the Club during my term of official service.

I appreciate your thoughtfulness.

With every good wish,

Sincerely,

Mr. Roswell Magill
President
The University Club
1 West 54th Street
New York 19, N.Y.

OFFICE OF THE VICE PRESIDENT
WASHINGTON, D. C.
February 1, 1961

Dear Mr. Magill:

Thank you very much for your letter of January 30.

I appreciate the kindness your club has extended me and I hope I will be able to enjoy its facilities before long.

Best regards.

Sincerely,

Lyndon B. Johnson

Mr. Roswell Magill, President
The University Club
One West Fifty-Fourth Street
New York 19, New York

For many years, it was the Club's practice to extend privileges to the president, vice president, cabinet secretaries and certain other officials during their terms of office. These are a few of the letters received from members of the newly installed Kennedy administration in 1961. How many people availed themselves of their privileges is unclear.

Notable Guests

Various

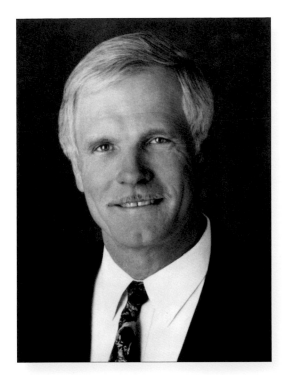

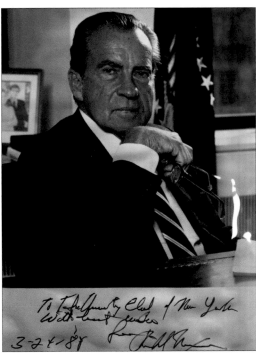

Top left: Robert Edward Turner III, the founder of CNN and a noted yachtsman, conservationist, philanthropist, and environmentalist, spoke at the Club in 1997. **Top right:** Former president Jimmy Carter spoke at the Club in 1991. **Bottom right:** Barbara Walters, whose distinguished career in broadcast journalism spans six decades, spoke at the Club in 2008. **Bottom left:** After former president Richard M. Nixon spoke at the Club in 1988, he sent this inscribed photograph.

Women in The University Club

The process of unwinding the men-only policy at the Club was a gradual one, and it required many decades to come to fruition. In 1932, the Club took the first step by inviting ladies to attend a recital and tea on the ground floor of the clubhouse. This was followed by other similar events. In January 1940, the rules were changed again, and ladies began to visit the clubhouse on Sunday evenings. In December of that year, the Club held its first dinner dance. The *New York Herald Tribune* took humorous note of this event.

In March 1942, the Club opened a new Ladies Dining Room on the ground floor, in the space formerly used for backgammon and now known as the Dwight Lounge. The plans for the new dining room show nine tables at the western side of the room, with the eastern side being taken up with a lounge area where people could enjoy their drinks. As the Club had few, if any, facilities for ladies, the room originally called "Strangers' Room" (and more recently "Visitors' Room") on the ground floor was converted into a ladies restroom.

The new dining room proved to be immensely popular, and by the end of 1942, 1,263 members had arranged for their wives to have cards giving them signing privileges. The fees for such cards, together with the revenue stream from the Ladies Dining Room, helped make the restaurant operation profitable.

That the Club would move in this direction was perhaps inevitable, given the way our society was evolving. In 1920, the Nineteenth Amendment to the U.S. Constitution guaranteed women the right to vote. Over time, all the colleges and universities whose shields adorn the façade of the clubhouse would become co-educational. Other New York City clubs were making similar accommodations. As the line from the old hymn reminds us,

New occasions teach new duties,
Time makes ancient good uncouth;

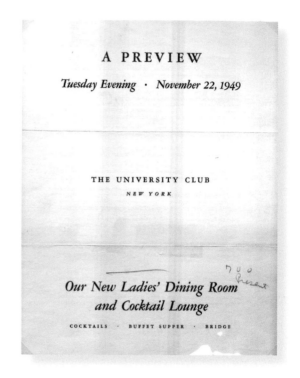

A PREVIEW

Tuesday Evening · November 22, 1949

THE UNIVERSITY CLUB
NEW YORK

*Our New Ladies' Dining Room
and Cocktail Lounge*

COCKTAILS · BUFFET SUPPER · BRIDGE

However, as to admitting women as members, 750 indicated approval of such a step, but 915 were opposed and 171 had no opinion.

In 1949, the Ladies Dining Room was moved into the space formerly used as the Grill (today the Dwight Dining Room). The Grill was moved to the mezzanine in place of billiards (which was displaced to the fifth floor). The space we know as the Dwight Lounge became a sitting area where drinks were served to women guests. In 1971, the Council decided that ladies might attend functions in the private dining rooms, and later that same year, members began to bring their wives with them to stay in the bedrooms on the third and sixth floors.

"My God! Already!" In its March 25, 1974, issue
The New Yorker *gently prodded the Club over its
then all-male policy.*

In 1977, the Club conducted a survey of its 3,750 members. In response to the general question of whether wives and female guests should have access to the clubhouse, 942 members said they should and 479 said no. With regard to separate questions about specific parts of the clubhouse, 736 members said that they were comfortable with women in the Library, but only 250 thought that women should visit the Tap Room, for instance.

However, as to admitting women as members, 750 indicated approval of such a step, but 915 were opposed and 171 had no opinion.

In 1980, the Council voted to admit women as members, but also sought the informal views of the membership. This provoked a sharp reaction from some members who styled themselves the "Committee of 100" and brought an action in New York State Supreme Court to compel the Council to submit the question to a vote of the membership. That vote, when held, rejected the admission of women by 1,143 to 608. There the matter rested until 1984, when the New York City Council passed Local Law 63, giving clubs the choice of admitting women or seeking to qualify under the "distinctly private" exception in the law. Three years later, once the law was upheld on appeal, the Club voted narrowly to become "distinctly private," meaning that no events for which the sponsoring member would be reimbursed by a business could be held in the clubhouse. The president of the Club, John Grant, who favored the admission of women, felt he could not continue to lead the Club given the way the vote went and resigned the presidency on February 1, 1987. Vice President Bruce Sargent became acting president. It was soon clear that "distinctly private" was a failure, and in another vote held in June 1987, the admission of women members was approved resoundingly. The first women were admitted later that year.

This decision set in train a number of alterations to the clubhouse. The first was the conversion of the former Ladies Dining Room and Lounge into the Dwight Room and Lounge (named for the first Club president, Theodore W. Dwight). Both spaces were completely redecorated, several new paintings were acquired for the walls, the furniture was replaced, and original doors that had languished in the basement for years were re-hung.

Accommodating women members in the athletic facilities was more of a challenge. As an interim step, a ladies locker room was created on the ninth floor for the use of squash players. For a time, the Club experimented with restricting access to the Fitness Center in the basement to women only during certain hours. When that proved impractical, for a few years, the Club would reimburse women for their dues at an outside fitness club if they joined one. In 2001, a Ladies Fitness Center and locker room was built on the eleventh floor. To make room for this facility, one singles squash court was removed and the space occupied by the laundry was reduced by one-half.

Today, a little over 12 percent of the membership are women. Not only are women involved in the leadership of the Club through serving on the Council and on committees, but a few have also been part of the place long enough to attend the annual dinner for twenty-five-year members. Their active participation contributes to the vibrancy of the Club, thereby ratifying the wisdom of the decision to admit women.

Beverly Sills

1982

The University Club
cordially invites you
to attend a

Gala Opera Evening

in honor of
Miss Beverly Sills
General Director, New York City Opera
on
Wednesday, April Seventh, Nineteen Hundred and Eighty-Two

In addition to her distinguished career as a soprano, Beverly Sills served as general director of the New York City Opera from 1979 to 1989, as president of Lincoln Center for the Performing Arts from 1994 to 2002, and as chairman of the Metropolitan Opera from 2002 to 2005. She died in 2007.

Justice Antonin Scalia

-115-

Associate Justice Antonin Scalia of the U.S. Supreme Court has twice spoken at The University Club, in 2004 and in 2014.

Walter Isaacson

-116-

Photo by Albert Watson

Club members Walter Isaacson and Jon Meacham have both earned Pulitzer Prizes for their distinguished work in the field of biography. Both have spoken at the Club on multiple occasions.

Jon Meacham

Celebratory Dinners

THE UNIVERSITY CLUB
Celebrating 150 Years

Committee Appreciation Dinner
Thursday, June 26, 2014

RECEPTION

Chef's Selections of Hot and Cold
Passed Hors d'oeuvres

DINNER

Seafood Salad
Shrimp, Scallop & Crab
Avocado & Citrus

Chateau Fuissé, Pouilly-Fuissé, "Le Clos," 2009

**

Medallions of Veal
Asparagus, Morels & Yukon Gold Mashed Potatoes

Domaine Bernard Rion, Vosne-Romanée, Les Chaumes, 1ᵉʳ Cru, 2002

**

English Summer Berry Pudding
Fromage Blanc Sorbet

Domaine du Pas Saint Martin, Coteaux du Layon, Les Mille Rocs, 2010

**

Coffee and Tea Service

THE UNIVERSITY CLUB
Celebrating 150 Years

25 Year Club

Thursday, October 17, 2013

Dinner Menu

Appetizer

Smoked Sable Tartine
Cucumber Salad

Campo al Mare Vermentino 2012

xoooooooox

Entrée

Grilled Bone-in Filet Mignon
Wild Mushrooms,
Tuscan Spinach, Herb Butter

Ch. Larose-Trintaudon Haut Medoc 2006

xoooooooox

Dessert

Milk Chocolate Tartlet
Green Tea Mousse and Roasted Apricot

Petits Fours & Chocolate Dipped Strawberries
Coffee & Tea Service

The custom of hosting a dinner to recognize members serving on all Club committees and the Council started in 2007, during the presidency of John Osnato. At each dinner, members rotating off committees are given a tie or a scarf as a token of appreciation.

The 25 Year Club honors members who have been a part of The University Club for that long, or longer. Upon reaching that milestone, each member receives a special pin. At every dinner, glasses inscribed with the Club logo and "The 25 Year Club" are distributed. A high point of the dinner is former Club president Jerome Coleman's monologue about events within and without the Club twenty-five years earlier.

V

THE LIBRARY

by Andrew Berner

"The promotion of literature and art, by establishing and maintaining a library, reading-room, and gallery of art...." Thus is the purpose of The University Club stated in its Charter, dated April 28, 1865. Though implying that a formal library was part of the Club from its inception, that does not appear to have been the case, though efforts were made to raise funds for "a Library of Reference" as early as November 1865. Still, there is nothing to indicate that one existed in the small brownstone at 9 Brevoort Place, the first home of The University Club. After two years there, the Club entered a twelve-year period during which there was no clubhouse, formal operations were suspended, and the charter was kept alive primarily through annual meetings.

In 1879, when the Club found its new home in the former Caswell mansion at the southwest corner of 35th Street and Fifth Avenue, among the first concerns of its newly expanded membership was the creation of a suitable library. Space was set aside on the second floor of the clubhouse, and in November 1879, the Council appointed a Committee on Literature and Art under the chairmanship of publisher Henry Holt. It wasn't long before Holt distributed to the membership a circular laying out what

Henry Holt

the Library should be, and soliciting support. In this circular, Holt noted that a library was "absolutely indispensable to [the Club's] equipment as a body composed of educated men." The solicitation raised some $3,500 from members, which was supplemented by contributions from the Club itself. The Library was underway.

At this time in its history, the Library's collections were available to members only for use in the clubhouse itself. Indeed, it would be the better part of a

Architect Charles McKim, recognizing the Library as the heart of the Club, had placed it on the central monumental floor of the three in the clubhouse.

century before efforts would be made to meet recreational reading needs (beyond "great standard works of literature") through a circulating collection.

In 1890—by which time the Club had moved to the former Jerome mansion at 26th Street and Madison Avenue—the collection numbered 8,000 volumes. *Harper's Weekly* noted that "the library [of The University Club] is the most extensive of all club libraries in the country." As early as June 1881, the first professional librarian had been hired by the Club, beginning an unbroken chain of professional

Opposite: The portal leading from the Library Atrium to the Main Room of the Library

management for the Library that continues to this day. By the time the Club moved to its present club-house in 1899, the collection had doubled in size to 16,000 volumes.

Architect Charles McKim, recognizing the Library as the heart of the Club, had placed it on the central monumental floor of the three in the club-house. Nonetheless, those visiting the Library in those first years at 54th Street would have seen a space far different from that existing today. It had always been McKim's intention to have the ceiling of the Library decorated. He knew that he wanted those decorations to be based on (and in some cases directly copied from) Pinturicchio's frescoes in the Borgia Apartments

H. Siddons Mowbray

of the Vatican. He also knew that he wanted to use artist H. Siddons Mowbray, with whom he had collaborated on the Frederick Vanderbilt home in Hyde Park. Initially, however, the Club chose not to pursue the decoration of the ceiling. It was not until 1902 that the Club agreed to commission Mowbray and to send him to Rome, and it was not until 1904 that the Library decorations as we know them today were completed and installed. The majority of the cost of this work was donated by Club member Charles T. Barney.

As the Club matured, the Library continued to grow, reaching 25,000 volumes in 1910. Other changes took place, as well. The year 1917 saw two events of particular significance. First, member Alonzo Barton Hepburn made a gift of stocks to the Club (with another following two years later), stipulating that they be sold and the proceeds used to create a fund, the income from which would be used "for the benefit of

the Library." Having previously covered all expenses involved in running the Library, the Club now found that some of those expenses could be covered through Hepburn Fund income. In future years, as generous members created additional funds through outright donations or bequests, more and more of the Library's operating expenses were covered through its

Alonzo Barton Hepburn

own income. Eventually, the Club agreed to cover all payroll-related expenses (along with facilities costs such as electricity, heat, furnishings, etc.), while the Library covered other operating expenses from its own income, the arrangement that remains in effect today.

Also in 1917, the Library was the recipient of a significant gift in kind when member Horace White left a collection of books relating to the subject of economics and economic history. While the Library had received individual volumes in the past, this appears to have been the first subject-specific collection donated to the Library. In the years to come, there would be many other books donated, both as gifts and bequests,

The Library in the 26th Street clubhouse

Above, clockwise from top left: Library Atrium, north aisle of Library Atrium, and Conversation Room (now Card Room), all circa 1900
Below: Cover, title page, and text page of bound volume of tributes to Librarian Mark Kiley on the occasion of his retirement

often including materials of a special nature. Many of these—along with books purchased for the collection—would become the future core of the Rare Book Collection and other Special Collections of the Library. By 1919, the total collections of the University Club Library stood at more than 36,500 volumes, a figure that would grow to more than 45,000 in 1930 and

nearly 60,000 in 1940, by which time the Library staff had increased to four.

From 1929 to 1962, the Library enjoyed a period of expansion not only in the extent of its collections, but also in the services provided to members. This was largely due to the presence of Librarian Mark Kiley, who served The University Club for all of those

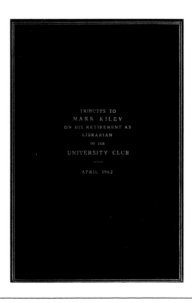
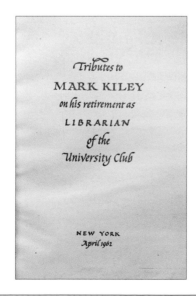
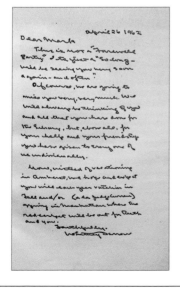

Top: Library ca 1900, prior to the decoration of the ceiling in 1904

Bottom: Illustration from Mark Catesby's Natural History… *showing the passenger pigeon*

Somerset Waters

thirty-three years, and whose leadership and management skills were exemplary. One way to measure the growing pride that members took in the Library was the marked increase in both monetary contributions and gifts of rare books and special collections that came in during the Kiley years. Within a decade of Kiley's retirement, the Club—facing the exigencies of the 1970s, a particularly difficult decade for clubs—reduced funding and staff for the Library. The result was a decline in services and in library use. The reversal of this trend came, appropriately, in 1979, the centennial of the initial organization of the Library by Henry Holt. The Library Committee, under the leadership of Somerset Waters, decided to bring in Guy St. Clair as Library Director, with the specific charge of revitalizing the Library and improving its services.

Also in 1979, Waters was able to secure funding for a Rare Book Room, in which the most significant volumes from the Library's collection could be

Architectural detail of the Library Atrium

properly housed and protected, while still being available for members to consult. Among the special treasures now housed in that space: the 1511 Ptolemy *Geographia*, with its early depiction of North America; the 1771 edition of Mark Catesby's remarkable *Natural History of Carolina, Florida and the Bahama Islands*; and Antonio Scaino's 1555 *Trattato del Giuco della Palla*, the first book printed on the subject of tennis. Also to be found are various Special Collections on subjects as varied as fine printing, antebellum Southern history, and George Cruikshank, to name but a few. In total, there are now approximately 9,000 titles in the Rare Book Room.

Among the many significant changes initiated by Guy St. Clair after his 1979 arrival, perhaps the most important was the creation, in 1982, of The University Club Library Associates. This was the first effort by any club library to create a "friends"

"Romance" by H. Siddons Mowbray adorns the east end of the Library

Library Associates tour to Sicily, 2010

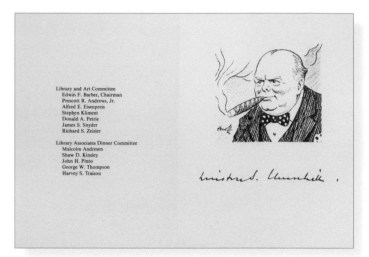

Library and Art Committee
Edwin F. Barber, Chairman
Prescott R. Andrews, Jr.
Alfred E. Eisenpreis
Stephen Kliment
Donald A. Petrie
James S. Snyder
Richard S. Zeisler

Library Associates Dinner Committee
Malcolm Andresen
Shaw D. Kinsley
John H. Pinto
George W. Thompson
Harvey S. Traison

The Library Associates is a group of University Club members who meet together to foster fellowship, interest in books and scholarship, and to encourage greater use of the Club's Library.

To commemorate Sir Winston Churchill's visit to the Club (on March 18, 1946), the Associates are delighted to have the Rt. Hon. Edward Heath, M.P., as guest speaker. Mr. Heath was educated at Balliol College, Oxford, where he was President of the University Conservative Association and President of the Oxford Union. He was elected to Parliament in 1950, and served as Minister of Labour in the government of Prime Minister Harold MacMillan. In October, 1964, Mr. Heath became a major opposition figure, leading his party to victory in the election of June, 1970, at which time he became Prime Minister.

An avid sportsman, Mr. Heath was the winner of the 1969 Sydney to Hobart Ocean Race and captained Britain's Admiral Cup Team in 1971 and 1979. He has written of his sailing adventures in *Sailing: A Course of My Life* (1975), and he has also written of his interest in music in *Music: A Joy for Life* (1976). He has been a member of the Council, Royal College of Music, Chairman of the London Symphony Orchestra Trust, Vice-President of the Bach Choir, and President of the European Community Youth Orchestra. Mr. Heath writes and speaks frequently on these subjects, as well as on politics and world affairs.

The Library Associates
of
The University Club
request the pleasure of your company
at
the Churchill Commemorative Dinner
and to hear a stimulating address by
the Rt. Hon. Edward Heath, M.P.
at the Club
on Tuesday, May 27th
at eight o'clock

R.S.V.P.   *Black Tie*
(card enclosed)

Cocktails in the Library at seven o'clock

group, not only to provide financial support, but also to provide a forum for Club members interested in books, literature, libraries and the like. A solicitation was sent to the membership in November 1982, and by the end of the year, there were 101 members. The group has continued to expand ever since, with membership now standing at approximately 1,500.

Throughout the history of the Associates, one of its most important aspects was the programming that it sponsored, bringing a variety of writers, poets, journalists, artists and others to speak at the Club and to provide a reason for Library Associates—and all

Above: Former Prime Minister Edward Heath with Library Director Guy St. Clair

members of the Club—to get together for social intercourse and intellectual stimulation. Speakers have included such prominent names as Simon Winchester, Terrence McNally, Susan Cheever, and Stephen Sondheim. In 1986, former British Prime Minister Edward Heath spoke at a Library-sponsored dinner marking the fortieth anniversary of Winston Churchill's 1946 speech at the Club.

Top left: The Card Room, 2014. Top right: Invitation to the 1986 dinner with Edward Heath, honoring the 40th anniversary of Winston Churchill's appearance at the Club.

Above: "Illumination," by H. Siddons Mowbray, one of four pendentives in the central dome of the Library

Beginning in 1986, an annual "Librarian's Lecture" has been given, and there have been many other programs and events too numerous to list ever since.

Among the most important points of maintaining the Library's legacy is a commitment to looking to the future while honoring the past. As early as 1980—a time when library automation was in its infancy—the Library closed its card catalog and began using computer-based cataloging. Over the intervening years, and in many small increments, technology has played a role in the evolution of the Library. More innovation no doubt awaits.

In the 1990s, the Library looked far beyond the walls of the clubhouse in providing a new service to members. A travel program was initiated, offering cultural tours, concentrating on the history, art, architecture and literature of a particular destination, with a strong emphasis on bibliographic treasures, as well. The funds that accrue to the Library as a result of these tours have enriched the Library's collections, through the purchase of over 120 volumes for the Rare Book Collection and other Special Collections.

Numerous publications have also originated in the Library, both in terms of writing and in terms of supervising publication. These have included works by Guy St. Clair, Percy Preston Jr., and Andrew Berner. In the spring of 2009, the Library also launched a new color periodical, *The Illuminator*, which has been very well received.

Today, the Library stands, in many ways, at a pinnacle. With approximately 100,000 volumes in the collection, it is—as it has been for some time—the largest private club library in the world. The University Club Library is second to none.

The sesquicentennial marks a significant milestone in the history of the Club and of the Library. But it is just that, a milestone on a road that has led up to this point, but which continues on into a future with, presumably, many more accomplishments still to come. It is hoped that the Library will continue to be seen as Henry Holt saw it in 1879, on the eve of its birth, as something that "will do more for [the Club's] reputation and permanence than any other possession could do."

VI

HIGHLIGHTS OF THE FINE ARTS COLLECTION

by Peggy Wunderlich

One of the stated purposes for the founding of the Club was to establish and maintain a "Gallery of Art." In 1884, the Yale alumni in the Club donated a portrait of Theodore Dwight Woolsey, president of Yale College, by Jonathan Eastman Johnson. This was the first in a collection of portraits of college and university presidents presented by alumni. Today, many of these pictures hang in the Main Dining Room. Nearby, in the Council Room, set into the paneling over the fireplace, hangs a portrait of Henry H. Anderson, president of the Club from 1879 to 1888, by George Bernard Butler. Anderson's portrait is the first of a retiring president commissioned by the Club, a tradition to this day.

In 1940, Edward Pearce Casey established a fund to acquire paintings by American artists. This has allowed the Club to expand the collection and, from time to time, commission new works. Over the years, the Club has benefited from numerous gifts of art—adding to our wonderful collection, which graces the Club walls today.

GEORGE GARDNER SYMONS, 1863–1930
Winter Scene with Cottages

Oil on Canvas
24 x 30 inches
Signed Gardner Symons left of center

Provenance:
Purchased Casey Fund from Sotheby Parke Bernet, Inc.
Fine Americana, 1979.

The Seventh Floor

George Gardner Symons's *Winter Scene with Cottages* is a fascinating combination of American Impressionism and Realism. Symons was a "plein-air" artist who executed his scenes outdoors, in situ, so he could capture the true light and weather conditions of the scene depicted. *Winter Scene with Cottages* reveals how successful this method was; the scene could be a rural wintry scene of today.

In addition to the lightened palette and play of light and shadow typical of Impressionism, Symons adds

Edward Pearce Casey

realistic details of everyday life: a woman, executed in a few strokes, comes out to collect the laundry drying on the line and in the foreground, snow-laden cottages are simple, rough affairs.

Born in Chicago, Illinois, between 1861 and 1863, Symons's original name was George Gardner Simon, changed to Symons due to anti-Semitism concerns. He studied at the Art Institute of Chicago, as well as in Paris, Munich and London. Symons had studios in Brooklyn, New York, and Laguna Beach, California, where he often painted with his lifelong friend, the landscape artist William Wendt. Symons was an Associate Member of the National Academy of Design, National Arts Club, California Art Club, etc. His works are in the collections of the Metropolitan Museum of Art, the Corcoran Gallery, and the Art Institute of Chicago, among others.

FREDERICK JUDD WAUGH 1861–1940
Yosemite, South Fork

Oil on Canvas
25 x 50 inches

Provenance:
Christie's Important American Paintings, Drawings and Sculpture, May 26, 1994.
Casey Fund
Robert Balshin, Larchmont, New York
Jeffrey Alan Gallery

The Dwight Lounge

Frederick Judd Waugh's great strength lies in his reductive, abstract compositions. These close-up snapshots of the natural world mark him as a 20th-century artist influenced by the relatively new art medium of photography. For *Yosemite, South Fork*, he concentrates on a close-up and simplified view of these mountains; the viewer sees them as a series of planes that use different shades of light to suggest depth, while the sharply defined angles convey the ruggedness of the terrain.

Son of the Philadelphia artist Samuel Waugh, he studied with Thomas Eakins and Thomas Anshutz at the Pennsylvania Academy of Art and with William Adolphe Bougereau at the Académie Julian in Paris. After Paris,

Waugh moved to the English island of Sark, part of the Channel Islands, where his interest in marine painting blossomed, inspired by the contrast of the sharp cliffs abutting the sea. During World War I, he was part of a group of marine camouflage artists. This group, under the aegis of the artist William Everett, covered the U.S. Navy's ships with Dazzle camouflage. Reportedly, only one such ship was lost. His works are in the collection of the Ulrich Museum, the Brooklyn Museum and the Smithsonian Institution, among others.

AUGUST BENZIGER
Theodore Roosevelt

Oil on canvas
Signed lower right

Provenance:
Museum of the Historical Society of Chicago
Exhibited in the Memorial Exhibition of August Benziger, 1867-1955, National Arts Club
Gift of Dr. Anton Pestalozzi, August 1991.

By the entrance to the Tap Room

Standing as if he were momentarily stopped, August Benziger's portrait of Teddy Roosevelt captures the tremendous vitality of the man. With his arms firmly grasping the top of the chair behind him and turned in this three-quarter pose to focus his intense scrutiny on us, we sense a man with little spare time. Benziger's treatment of Roosevelt's clothing is sumptuously painted, revealing subtle variations of the grey tonalities and the rich stuffs of his suit. By contrast, the handling of his face is quite different, composed of rough impasto suggesting a coarse, ruddy complexion.

Born in Switzerland, Benziger emigrated to America in 1852. His father, who had wanted August to pursue a career in chemistry, was head of a renowned publishing company whose clients included the papacy. So when Benziger switched to art after studying in Paris with William Bougereau and Leon Bonnat at the École des Beaux Arts, his father's connections would have provided him with a ready supply of patrons. Following his father to New York City, Benziger became a portrait painter whose subjects included Presidents McKinley and Taft, as well as Roosevelt, Thomas Edison and Pope Leo XIII.

PIETER CASTEELS III, 1684–1749
*A Still Life of Tulips, Peonies, an Iris and Other Flowers in a Vase Resting
on a Stone Ledge*

Oil on Canvas
29 x 24 inches
Signed and dated 1733

Purchased Raphael Vallis Limited
London, January 2002
Exhibited "Nature's Image," Newhouse Galleries, New York
May 11th to June 17th, 1988

The Dwight Dining Room

This still life painting by Pieter Casteels is a virtuoso example of the genre. The collection of flowers almost fills the frame, nature's bounty spilling out of the vase that holds them. Casteels creates a repetition of color, red tones versus whites to move the eye through the painting. Note his delights in the linear–a Parrot Tulip's leaves are curled back to reveal the dying flower. Casteels uses his talent to detail each petal and revel in depicting each flower in its unique beauty.

Born in Antwerp into a family of painters, son of Pieter Casteels II and Elizabeth Bosschaert, he migrated to England in 1708 and remained there for the rest of his life. He was a noted painter of decorative, floral and bird still lifes. He painted an important series, "The Twelve Months of Flowers," for Robert Furber of Kensington, which became a popular subject for both needlepoint and tapestry. He retired from painting in 1735.

WILLARD METCALF, 1858–1925
Late Afternoon in March, Chester, Vermont

Oil on canvas
Purchased, Casey Fund, 1967
The Seventh Floor

Late Afternoon in March is one of the Club's most impressive pieces of American Impressionism. Considered to be the master of New England winter scenes, Metcalf, in this painting, perfectly captures winter's cool, ethereal, beauty. No people or their detritus detract from the spare, snowy scene. Instead, Metcalf delights in the use of light and shade to delineate the delicate tracery of

the tree's shadows on the snow. In turn, these shadows lead the eye over the empty foreground space to the houses and hills of the background, while the predominance of blue tonalities in the palette convey the cold temperatures. American Impressionists held on to reality, and painted the scene rather than the "impression." They sought, as Metcalf here achieves, to depict a realistic outdoor scene.

Metcalf was a member of The Ten, a group of artists who left the Society of American Artists to pursue American Impressionism. The group comprised many of the other major American Impressionists such as Childe Hassam, John Henry Twachtman, and Thomas Wilmer Dewing. Metcalf was also part of the Old Lyme Artists Colony. Interested in naturalism, he spent summers in Connecticut painting and collecting bird eggs and nests. He resided and painted in Cornish, New Hampshire, and also in Vermont and Maine. *Late Afternoon in March* was included in an exhibit by Milch Galleries of the Chester, Vermont paintings in 1923. Metcalf's paintings are in the collections of the Art Institute of Chicago, the Corcoran Gallery of Art, the Freer Collection, the Metropolitan Museum of Art and the National Gallery of Art, among others.

3.

2.

6.

5.

Above, examples of original furniture designed by McKim, Mead & White for The University Club

VII

DECORATIVE ARTS IN THE UNIVERSITY CLUB
by Timothy R. Hamilton

In an organization such as The University Club, furniture and related arts such as lighting serve a clear purpose, just as they do in everyday houses, but on a grander scale: that is, to provide a practical means for seating, dining, reading, games or just lounging about. The myriad of chairs, sofas, settees, clocks, tables of all sizes and shapes, sconces, chandeliers, floor and table lamps, whether grand or incidental, have all contributed to members' comfort and to our interior decoration through the years. But some of our furnishings seem to play a double role as "ornaments" to the clubhouse, in many cases as an extension and amplification of McKim, Mead & White's architecture. The members of the firm were conscious of this role often played by movable furnishings. All three principals of the firm, Charles Follen McKim, Stanford White, and William Mead, in addition to William Kendall of the firm, were members of The University Club. While

Stanford White

McKim was the lead architect of the project, it seems not unlikely that all the partners worked together in degrees to form the 54th Street building and its interiors. Stanford White was known in particular for having a penchant for furniture and decoration, and considered these of great importance in the firm's architectural commissions.

Furniture and Decorative Arts for the Club

The most important group of furnishings and light fittings discussed here are those which the architects designed or had made for the 54th Street building. An article written by Channing Blake for *The Magazine Antiques*,[1] details some of The University Club's original furnishings designed by McKim, Mead & White, along with a discussion of pieces designed by other prominent firms for a handful of American Beaux Arts buildings. Another exceptionally informative article was written by Andrew Berner, current Library Director and Curator of Collections, in the form of an inventory and report prepared for the Library & Art Committee in 1997.[2] The Club's archives also contain many photographs of room interiors ranging from just after the building was opened in 1899 up to the present time, showing the evolution of each.

Most of the original architect-designed furniture of the Club was made by an eponymous New York firm called T.D. Wadleton. In his article, Channing Blake refers to Wadleton as a "cabinetmaker," mentions that he had been a draftsman at the McKim, Mead & White firm for a brief period, and that he had, working for them and for other architectural firms, provided newly made historicist furniture for the houses of such clients as Henry W. Poor, Charles T. Barney (instrumental in his role as Chairman of the Building Committee for the 54th Street clubhouse), William C. Whitney, Payne Whitney, Levi P. Morton, Clarence MacKay and others, as well as for organizations such as The Morgan Library, the Union Club, the Yale Club, the Knickerbocker Trust Company and the Madison Square Presbyterian

[1] Blake, Curtis Channing, "Architects as Furniture Designers," in *The Magazine Antiques*, vol. CXXVIII, no. 5 (May 1976), p. 1042.
[2] Berner, Andrew, "Original Furniture of The University Club," Sept. 1997.

Church.[3] Mosette Broderick, a McKim scholar, refers to T.D. Wadleton as "a professional decorator" and states that he, at least at the time of furnishing the Payne Whitney house (circa 1906), shared the same street address as the architects.[4] Whatever Wadleton's exact status, it seems clear that he was able to carry out the wishes of demanding architects who extended their design influence through to the late stages of furnishing and interiors for projects, as was done at The University Club.

The Club's Main Reading Room along Fifth Avenue contains a trove of original furniture designed by the architects in a variety of historicist styles, but with combinations of eclectic decorative details making them late-19th-century creations of their very own. The writing desks, from the double-sided examples with stationery racks, to the larger and smaller single desks (Fig. 1) are part of this original group, as are the giltwood marble-top console tables and long Louis XIV-style sofas against the west walls, and the two massive tables, one at each end of the room. The two different sets of armchairs against the windows, one set *en suite* with the sofas (Fig. 2), were also designed for the building.

After more than a century, and with changes in social conventions and ways of using furniture, some pieces have moved from room to room. The massive carved walnut Elizabethan-style vase-leg table

4.

1.

at the south end of the Reading Room (Fig. 3) and the armchairs with twisted stretchers (Fig. 4) were originally made for the Council Room, as seen in early photographs. The other massive table on the north end of the Reading Room, built of oak and used to display daily newspapers (Fig. 5), has boldly scrolled, arcaded and fluted trestle supports and is executed in a more strict Italian Renaissance style; it seems always to have been in the room. This piece is very closely related to another grand table which is located in the Conference Room on the third floor and used by members for meetings; it differs only slightly from its Reading Room cousin in the carved decorative detail, and was originally made for the fourth floor Periodical Room in the Library.

The pair of handsome, well-proportioned giltwood console tables on the west walls of the Reading Room (Fig. 6) (together with a matching third table now placed elsewhere) were designed for this space. These tables, originally four in number, are excellent examples of the eclectic furniture designs of McKim, Mead & White—rooted in a solid, architectonic classicism,

---

[3] Blake. *op cit.*

[4] Broderick, Mosette Glaser, *Triumvirate: McKim, Mead & White: Art, Architecture, Scandal and Class in America's Gilded Age*, New York, Alfred P. Knopf, 2010, p. 481.

[5] By the end of the 19th century, even some grandly scaled furniture was being constructed in a more expedient manner than seen in the 17th and 18th centuries, where joints would have been of the more complex (and durable) mortise-and-tenon type. These tables, like much of the furniture created for the building by Wadleton, are put together using wood dowels.

[6] Curiously, all the rear legs on this pair of side tables seem to be cut out to be accommodated in a very specific location in the Club, probably being at one time nearly built onto the paneling and moldings of an architectural wainscot.

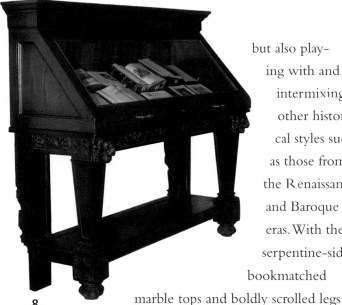

8.

but also playing with and intermixing other historical styles such as those from the Renaissance and Baroque eras. With their serpentine-sided bookmatched marble tops and boldly scrolled legs ending in paw feet, they exhibit design motifs repeated in variations many times in the Club's original furniture. In 2012, these tables were fully restored, curing structural fatigue,[5] broken marble, and missing stretcher elements, as well as to recreate their partially burnished gilded surfaces.

In the Club's Main Atrium, architect-designed furniture includes the pair of classical-style side tables (Fig. 7), solidly made of oak and with mottled green marble tops. The legs again exhibit bold molded scrolls, this time ending in cast bronze paw feet. We see in circa 1900 photographs that these tables were first used in the Club's original Conversation Room on the fourth floor (now the Card Room).

Traveling upward to the fourth floor of The University Club, home of the Library, Conversation and Card Rooms, one encounters another rich grouping of furniture and decorative arts supplied specifically for the building. The Library Atrium contains a pair of mahogany console tables (with later-added display vitrine tops) probably designed by McKim, Mead & White (Fig. 8) in a Regency style particularly inspired by—but not copying—Thomas Hope, the great furniture designer of early 19th century England. The Club's versions are, not surprisingly, gutsy and inventive—the heavy classical tables make use of scrolling acanthus

friezes and lion's head masks carved in high relief. The tapering paneled legs, however, retain the more Victorian detail of incised blocks carved with four corner spandrels, a detail also seen on the legs of the massive tables in the west and east rooms of the Library, all designed *en suite*.[6]

The Library Atrium also contains four large green-glazed pottery jars, probably of late 19th century origin, inspired by ancient examples, which hold potted palms (see p. 123). Though certainly not made by Wadleton, the jars must have been approved by the architects, or at least seen by of them. Together with their Chinese export marble-inset carved rosewood stands,[7] they are today used along the Atrium's north aisle, as also seen in circa 1900 photographs. These jars have, over the years, spent time in other locations including the Main Dining Room and at the edge of the pool in the Men's Fitness Center.

The Main Room of the Library is, like the first-floor Reading Room, full of original, architect-designed or specified furnishings. The pair of monumental oak book tables, which artfully mix Baroque and Classical details, all in the guise of a Renaissance refectory table form (see foldout p. 125), exhibit similar design elements to the writing desks on the first floor, again showing bold scrolled legs, carved end panels and leafy feet. The book-rack superstructures are modern, built of

7.

---

[7] Three of the Chinese stands seem to be originally associated with the pots; the fourth stand also dates from circa 1900, but was acquired at auction in recent years to replace a broken original, and differs only slightly from the others in the carved detail. Such stands, their tops often inset with marble, were made in large quantities in China through the Victorian period and beyond, specifically for export to Western markets.

9.

10.

11.

These sturdy and useful tables are very much favored by members, who use them daily while enjoying the Library; they match well with their original mahogany armchairs (Fig. 11), designed in a restrained Regency style with reeded legs and partially caned backrests.

Also on the Library floor are a large group of low-slung leather-upholstered oak armchairs with molded and scrolled arm terminals used for lounging or reading (Fig. 12); these chairs seem to be identical to those once located in the very-densely-furnished Main Atrium, arranged around the interior perimeter of that space along with more incidental pieces, such as the numerous small oak tripod cocktail tables and porters' benches still to be found throughout the building today.

The fourth floor of The University Club, because it is used so rarely for events which necessitate the clearing–out of furniture, has been a landing place for other original furnishings, such as a set of dining chairs created originally for the enfilade of Private Dining Rooms on the ninth floor (and visible in early photographs). James W. Alexander writes that the interior decoration of this suite of private dining rooms was "designed and executed by W. Francklyn Paris, architect."[8] These chairs (Fig. 13) were made to evoke the style of the late 17th century Anglo-Dutch reign of William and Mary, their arched and scrolled backrests partially caned and carved with flowerheads and fruit, above block-and-turned arms and legs. Today, chairs from

well-chosen oak in a sympathetic style for the 2012 Library renovation; they also act as supports for the disguised, powerful uplights of bronzed metal which serve to illuminate the Library ceiling. The circular table below the central dome of the Library (see p. 120) is made of well-figured mahogany in a weighty Neoclassical style, perhaps inspired by designs of Robert and James Adam, the English brothers who revived ancient motifs unearthed in the 18th century excavations of Herculaneum and Pompeii. The legs are carved with swagged urns, husks and ram's head elements, heightened with gilding. Early photographs show this large table, at the time without any bookrack, positioned in the middle of the Library Atrium.

More straight-laced and also designed by McKim, Mead & White are the matching library writing tables (Fig. 9), located in most bays of the room. Built of solid mahogany, these handsome tables exist in several sizes, and have legs inlaid at the top with marquetry Classical urns (Fig. 10) and carved with restrained fluting as they taper down to bronze caps at the feet. This is a rare example of decorative inlay used on furniture in the Club. Nearly all other pieces rely upon carving for their embellishment.

[8] Alexander, James W., *A History of The University Club of New York 1865–1915*, Charles Scribner's Sons, New York, 1915, p. 220. Alexander calls William Francklyn Paris an "architect," and this is another indication that McKim, Mead & White involved consultants for some of their project interiors, just as they did with T.D. Wadleton for furniture and E.F. Caldwell for lighting. William Francklyn Paris was the author of the book *Decorative Elements in Architecture: Random observations on the fitness of things from a decorative point of view* (New York: John Lane Co., 1917), which advocated, in an almost zealot-like, way for suitable interior architecture making use of historical ornament to embellish or furnish newly built rooms.

12.

13.

this original large set are to be found on the fourth floor and also in other locations throughout the clubhouse.

While the seventh floor Council Room and Breakfast Room have for many years been kept free of permanent furniture, the Main Dining Room contains a further grouping of McKim, Mead & White-designed and other related decorative arts. The most prominent of these are the pair of massive oak sideboard tables essentially built onto the north wall of the Dining Room (Fig. 14). These are three tiers high, the fronts with bold lion monopodia supports cast in plaster, and were designed by the firm and made by T.D. Wadleton for the room. Now restored, these are to be seen as an extension of the architecture itself, and continue to this day to serve as useful pieces in the service of food and drink to members. As is the case with these and other grand, original pieces of furniture discussed in this chapter, their mass and scale can stand up to the huge rooms for which they were made.

14.

While it is unclear exactly when the colorful embroidered and appliquéd velvet banner (Fig. 15) above the Dining Room fireplace appeared, it was certainly custom-made for the club building, either right from the start or in the early 20th century. It depicts the Club's shield within an Italianate cartouche, the cyphcred letters "UC" and "NY" alternating at each corner, all within a foliate scroll border. Directly below the banner is a gilt and patinated bronze mantel garniture of a clock and pair of electrified candelabra, dating from the late 19th century (Fig. 15), presumably purchased or otherwise acquired for the building around 1900, but not designed specifically for it. Typical of three-piece mantel garnitures of the time, it is cast and chased in a classical revival style, probably in France, and retailed by Tiffany & Co., who brought to the New York market the kinds of elaborate and luxurious room decorations demanded by their patrons.

15.

16.

17., 18.

19.

Edward F. Caldwell & Co. Lighting Fixtures in The University Club

The famed New York firm of Edward F. Caldwell & Co.[9] were designers and makers of some of the most inventive, high-quality light fittings and metal decorative arts ever produced in America, and they supplied the majority of original light fixtures and other metalwork[10] in The University Club.

As lighting designers, Caldwell worked with many prominent architectural firms on a myriad of well-known private and public projects, from various mansions and clubs, to the New York Public Library and The White House in the 1902 renovations.

Lighting fixtures designed and made for The University Club in cast and patinated bronze (and designed to be fitted for electricity) include the set of massive foliate-scrolled Classical wall lights cast with masks in the Main Reading Room (Fig. 16) and the numerous bronze table lamps cast "after the ancient" also in the room; the Anglo-Dutch sconces and chandeliers (Figs. 17 and 19), and the wall lights with favrile glass shades (Fig. 18) located throughout the Library; the Neoclassical sconces with upturned serpents (see p. 123) and a pair of majestic paw-foot floor torchieres in the Library Atrium (see p. 120). Also notable are the Baroque-style monumental bronze chandeliers and wrought iron foliate-scrolled wall lights of the Main Dining Room (Fig. 20), and related examples in the Council Room[11] and a number of other fixtures throughout the Club. All the Club's original Caldwell lighting fixtures, whatever their historic style inspiration, exhibit bold, gutsy forms updated for then-novel Edison bulbs and have crisply cast decorative detail based on historic European models, of which the firm kept a formidable collection.

[9] The Edward F. Caldwell & Co. Collection is held at the Cooper-Hewitt Museum Library in New York, which is part of the Smithsonian Institution Libraries. This massive archive, available online, consists of over 50,000 images of photographs or original design drawings of lighting and other objects produced by the company during its existence. Some entries include account or other reference numbers which can be linked to specific architects or their projects.

[10] The wrought metal demilune-shaped grille directly above the Club's front door, worked with rosettes and curled leaf designs, is a good example of architectural metalwork made by Edward F. Caldwell & Co. for the Club, as distinct from lighting. This element, or an identical one, is photographed in the Caldwell Archives as no. A-49793.

20.

21.

22.

Edward F. Caldwell & Co. also designed and made some furniture and small decorative arts, and there is one notable non–lighting piece in The University Club which seems to be attributable to the firm: the marble console table (Fig. 21) in the elevator foyer of the Main Dining Room on the seventh floor. An identical table is pictured in the Caldwell archives (Fig. 22)[12]; however, the Club's table has two collection labels on the under-side stating that it was donated in either 1960 or 1961. The well-carved white marble trestle supports are archi-tectural in nature and boast the bold scrolled outlines so familiar in the Club's furniture, embellished with a rich Classical vocabulary of ornament such as satyrs' masks, leaf-and-berry festoons, fluting and acanthus leaf borders, taken from ancient sources. The supports are united with a long piece of colored specimen marble forming the tabletop. Such marble furnishings may well have been produced in Italy to be imported and/or retailed by Caldwell.

Other Furniture and Decorative Arts

While a great majority of the furnishings of The University Club were made for its building as designed by McKim, Mead & White, there are a handful of other pieces which were either acquired as antique during the early days of the 54th Street clubhouse (even moved from 26th Street), or which have been acquired recently with the spirit of the building in mind. There is a white marble and carved giltwood Neoclassical console table at the east end of the Main Dining Room which is notable, being from much earlier in the 19th century than the building (Fig. 23). Also, the set of good–quality ormolu wall sconces and the large chandelier of gilt bronze and cut glass in the Dwight Lounge on the first

---

[11] The fixtures in the Council Room have been altered at some time in the past. They have lost their cluster bulbs, and now have large flared shades.

[12] The photograph in the Caldwell archive shows a table with identical carved supports but with a temporary plank top. The club's table has a marble top and collection labels which state that the original owner was a Colonel E.R. Bradley, who bought the piece in Italy, and that it was then donated to the Club by Mrs. E.R. Williams in either 1960 or 1961.

23.

24.

25.

floor were bought as part of the renovation of that anteroom to what was then known as the Ladies Dining Room.

One notable piece purchased by the Club relatively recently, in 2006, is the large English mahogany center table (Fig. 24) in the Main Atrium, which dates from the period of George IV, circa 1825. This room was once much more fully furnished, including with a large circular writing table as shown in early photographs. Through the years a desire developed to locate a table which could evoke the earlier arrangement (though dispensing with Victorian clutter), and the Club was able to purchase this table at auction after a long search. The table is inspired by Thomas Hope, the English Regency designer earlier mentioned as a source for McKim, Mead & White's furniture. Carved with a variety of Classical running ornament such as egg-and-dart, beading and lotus leaves, it is supported on a tripod plinth with demonstrative winged animal paw feet.

Another piece of recently acquired American "Beaux Arts" furniture, bought at auction in 2011, is

a mahogany and bronze firescreen dating from circa 1895 (Fig. 25). Located in front of the fireplace in the east room of the Library in the winter, the screen also is used decoratively to fill the opening of the massive Main Dining Room fireplace during the summer months, when fires are not lit. The piece exhibits a variety of Classical ornament in the manner of McKim, Mead & White, such as fluted, leafy columns, applied carving of rosettes and palmette vines, and a scrolled cresting and feet; the bronze center panel is pierced with foliage and wreaths.

Exactly how much extant furniture was moved from the Club's previous home at the Jerome Mansion on 26th Street is unknown. The figured mahogany tallcase clock in our Main Atrium (Fig. 26) was likely moved to 54th Street from there, given that the clock, or one exceptionally similar, appears in a rare photograph of the front hall of the 26th Street clubhouse. With an impressive height of nearly nine feet, this clock dates from the Gothic Revival period, circa 1845, and may be of New York origin. Though the clock case is

26.

27.

28.

not in the best of condition, it exhibits good elements of the Gothic style in its pointed arch hood and spire finial. A further refinement is that this timepiece is a "regulator," the steel dial, double mercury pendulum and mechanical movement having a complexity beyond a regular clock.

It is possible that the thirty-inch terrestrial floor globe (Fig. 27) now located in the Card Room was moved from the old clubhouse. Made by the well-known "Geographers, Engravers & Printers" W & A.K. Johnston of Edinburgh, it seems to date from the very end of the 19th century. If not moved to 54th Street, it would have been acquired early on for the new building, because James W. Alexander in his history makes mention of "the great globe of the world"[13] when he describes McKim's new Library spaces. A photographic view of the Jerome mansion library (see p. 122) exists,[14] and in the grainy distance is a floor globe of seemingly similar height, silhouette and overall style—perhaps the very same globe.

Another surviving piece of furniture from a Club room no longer existing is a planked side chair (Fig. 28) carved in Dutch vernacular style (located for years in the washroom on the fourth floor). When the Club's

Annex was built around 1916, the entire extreme northwest corner of the existing building was demolished to make way for the architectural grafting-on of the addition—one of the rooms lost was the fifth floor Pipe Room. This room, used by members for smoking, was decorated in the somewhat romanticized Dutch 17th century style of the day; this charming small chair is the sole survivor of the Pipe Room.

This overview of furnishings of The University Club, whether they are historic or more recently acquired, should result in a reaffirmation of members' appreciation for the variety of decorative arts owned by the Club. While only a selection of furniture and light fittings were able to be presented in this volume, and while some pieces have obviously been lost over the years (as tastes change and pieces simply wear out), several things should be clear: that the Club in its 150th year of existence should be proud that it has held on to a great deal of the original furniture designed by McKim, Mead & White for its impressive building, and that some pieces have been well restored, and the Club continues on that pathway as we are able. Above all, we, as members of The University Club, are privileged to continue using and enjoying these interesting furnishings within their beautiful surroundings, as was the original intent.

[13] Alexander, *op. cit.*, p. 267.

The club's other large floor globe, with lion mask ornaments and located in the Library's main room, did not enter the Club's collection until 1963, as the gift of member K. Bruce Mitchell. As explained in an archived curatorial note authored by former Club Librarian Guy St. Clair, the globe was originally specified by architect William Wells Bosworth for the Boardroom of his handsome, classical American Telephone & Telegraph Company building at 195 Broadway, completed in 1916. It passed through several other owners and was eventually presented to Mr. Mitchell, who gave it to The University Club.

[14] Alexander, *op. cit.*, illustrated opposite p. 20.

VIII

SQUASH AT THE UNIVERSITY CLUB OF NEW YORK

by James Zug

For people in the small but passionate world of squash, The University Club of New York is an icon. Since it took up the game nearly a century ago, the Club is widely viewed as one of the most important facilities in the country. Moreover, unlike some other major clubs, it has been visionary and progressive, constantly pushing for change, even while retaining its traditional old-world charm and exclusivity.

The Club opened its first squash courts in 1918 and almost immediately assumed the leadership of the game in New York City. Under the direction of member Arthur H. Lockett, NY Squash (then called the Metropolitan Squash Racquets Association) first convened at 1 West 54th Street. Soon the Club began to host the annual city championships (the actual draw of the first tournament hangs on the wall outside the showcase singles court). The University Club was a natural stop for touring sides and the location for Lockett's eponymous seven-man, inter-city competition between New York, Boston and Philadelphia that compared only to the national championship in importance. Lockett, ever extraordinary, also persuaded the Club to build a squash doubles court in 1928 and inaugurated it in January 1929 with the world's first doubles tournament, another eponymous tournament (the Lockett Cup Invitational Doubles, a popular event that lasted until the late 1950s). In addition to Lockett, the Club has served as the home for generations of leaders in the game: most of the NY Squash presidents in its first half-century were University Club members. Current NY Squash President Steven Carter and two recent U.S. Squash Board Chairmen, John Fry and Peter Lasusa, are members of the Club.

George E. Cummings (right) was hired as a Locker Room Boy in 1919. Responsible for training many of New York City's leading squash players, George was the Club's first full-time Squash Professional. He held this position from 1920 to 1962. The Club's doubles court was inaugurated on November 9, 1928.

Throughout its history, The University Club has led from the front. It continued to host major tournaments—it was the headquarters for the 1940, 1950, 1957 and 1966 U.S. men's national singles, and thus witnessed some of the most memorable matches in that event's long history. Over the years, many leading champions have played there, as well. The membership roster has included U.S. Squash Hall of Famers Ned

Amidst great fanfare, The University Club hosted the first American Open Singles Squash Racquets Championship on January 1–5, 1954 (hardball). The concept of US Squash Racket Championships (now known as the US Open Squash Championships) originated with Club member Edwin "Ned" Bigelow. Pictured above is Hall of Fame player Hashim Khan (left) playing against Club Head Squash Professional (1978–1984), Douglas McLaggen (right). Hashim lost in the finals to Henri Salaun 3–0 (15–7; 15–12; 15–14) in front of a packed gallery of 250 spectators (the grand prize was $500, ticket price $23 for a seat, $3.45 standing room). The Club hosted the US Open again in 1963.

Edwards and Kenton Jernigan, and National Champion Jeff Stanley. Among its illustrious Head Professionals, the great Scotsman Douglas McLaggan was a U.S. Open Semi-Finalist, and Canadian, Gary Waite and Australian, Damien Mudge dominated the professional doubles tour, including numerous North American Opens, during their tenures at the Club.

Unusual for a facility of its stature, the Club has always encouraged younger players. As juniors in the 1920s, brothers Larry and Beek Pool learned the game from pro George Cummings; each went on to star at Harvard and win the U.S. Nationals twice. In 1939, the Club started the world's first invitational tournament for collegiate players, a classic holiday

event; and in 1988, it revived the National Intercollegiate Doubles and hosted it for a quarter-century.

The biggest milestone for squash at The University Club came in 1954 when the Club hosted the inaugural United States Open, the nation's first prize-moneyed singles event open to both amateurs and professionals. The Open, which the Club hosted for its first three years and again in 1963, was a watershed moment for squash in the country. The Club got more attention in the press from those first three days in early January 1954—including a large spread in *Life* magazine and a front-page, above-the-fold photograph and article in *The New York Times*—than any squash event in the United States had ever received up to that point. Four years later, the Club's squash courts were again highly visible: the February 1958 *Sports Illustrated* featured squash players on its cover in a photograph taken on The University Club's showcase singles court.

In doubles, the Club has been equally innovative. The O'Reilly Pro–Am is the oldest and most presti-

On April 18, 2011, The University Club hosted the men's "Players Championship," where Damien Scott Mudge (near right) and Ben Gould (far left) defeated Clive Leach (near left) and Matt Jensen (far right) 3–0. Mudge, the Head Squash Professional at the Club from 2001 to present, initially played right wall with former Club Head Professional (from 1999 to 2005) Gary Waite. As a team, Waite and Mudge had four undefeated seasons and were the No. 1 world-ranked doubles squash team for six seasons. Pictured below with right-wall partner Gould, Damien continued his dominance of the doubles tours with eleven years on the No. 1 world-ranked doubles team with various partners. Legendary referee Larry Sconzo is pictured in the upper right-hand corner on the Referee Chair.

gious professional-amateur doubles event in the country. Founded in 1943, it is a flagship event on the North American Professional Doubles Circuit. The Club has also hosted numerous professional events like the Kellner Cup and the World Doubles, as well as the U.S. national doubles in 1956, 1979, 2002, 2005 and 2014. In addition, the Silver Fox, named for Howard Story, was started in 1981 and thus is one of the older and most important of the member-guest tournaments in the country.

During the last decade, the Club has become a haven for women's squash, hosting leagues and tournaments and becoming the home for the best female singles and doubles players in New York City. In addition, the Club has helped establish the fact that squash is a lifetime sport by leading the launch of a new U.S. Squash-sanctioned national championship, the Century, which since its creation, in 2008, has become one of the most popular doubles events in the country. Arguably, no other sport plays as large and as cohesive a role among members as squash—which is why the tenth floor remains one of the most important areas in our gorgeous building.

70th O'Reilly, 2013 finals: James Brown (left) and Chris Walker (right-center) defeated Ahmed Anvari (left-center) and Andrew Zimmerman (right) 3–1 (15–5, 9–15, 15–9, 15–10).

The facilities on the tenth floor have evolved quite a bit from the original two cement-glazed courts opened in 1918. In 1923, the Club erected three more hardball singles courts. Five years later, it added two more and a doubles court. In 1939, the original 1923 courts were remodeled, with large viewing galleries installed. The facilities remained the same until 1997 and 1999, when in two phases the Club remodeled the tenth floor to make six softball singles courts and one doubles court.

George Cummings arrived as a locker-room attendant in 1919 and soon became the new Squash Professional. Cummings, working at the Club until 1966, was a landmark figure in the game of squash. He was succeeded by John Greco, a former weight-lifter and pro at the City Athletic Club. In 1978, Greco was succeeded by Doug McLaggan who stayed until 1985, earning just the second testimonial dinner, after Cummings, in the Club's long history. Larry Hilbert then came in 1985, followed by J.D. Cregan from 1989 until 1997, and then Gary Waite from 1997 to 2001. In 2001, Damien Mudge, who originally arrived at the Club as Waite's assistant in 1998, took over as Head Professional and began to make a dent on Cummings' perhaps unassailable record of forty-seven years of service.

On April 18, 2011, The University Club hosted the women's "Players Championship." The 2010 WDSA winners, Narelle Krizak (near left) and Susie Pierpont (near right), successfully defended their title as the number one world's women's doubles team by defeating fomer world singles #1, Natalie Grainger (far left) and U.S. Singles #1, Amanda Sobhey (far right) 3–2 (15–10; 17–18; 15–8; 9–15; 15–5). Referee Larry Sconzo is pictured in the °upper right-hand corner on the Referee Chair.

THE TRADITION OF SQUASH AT
THE UNIVERSITY CLUB OF NEW YORK

"For people in the small, but passionate world of squash, The University Club of New York is an icon. Since it took up the game nearly a century ago, the Club has been viewed as one of the most important squash venues in the country. Moreover, it has, unlike many of the other major clubs, been visionary, constantly pushing for progressive change, even while retaining its traditional, old-world charm."

—*James Zug, author:* Squash: A History of the Game *(Scribner, 2003)*

Milestones:

1918 – Club opens its first squash courts, New York Squash (then called the Metropolitan Squash Racquets Association) first convened at the Club and soon the Club began to host the annual New York City Championships.

1926 – Hosts inaugural U.S. vs. Canada Challenge Matches now known as the "Lapham-Grant" (also hosted in '44)

1928 – Installs doubles court, along with two additional singles courts

1929 – Hosts the world's first squash doubles tournament

1939 – Hosts inaugural Collegiate Invitational Tournament

1940 – Hosts first National Championship (also hosted in '50, '57 and '66)

1943 – Begins annual hosting of O'Reilly Pro-Am Doubles Championships

1954 – Hosts inaugural U.S. Open Squash Championships (also hosted in '55, '56 and '63)

1961 – Inaugural Bigelow Cup Inter-Club Doubles Championships vs. Union Club and Racquet & Tennis Club

1988 – Begins twenty-eight-year run hosting National Intercollegiate Doubles Championships

1997 – Inaugural David B. Hill Memorial Class "D" Doubles Championship

1999 – Remodeling of the singles courts completed

1999 – Inaugural Club Century Cup Doubles Championship for the Howe Trophy

1999 – Hosts Inaugural Kellner Cup Pro Doubles Championship

2001 – Hosts National Doubles Championships (also hosted in 2004 and 2014)

2002 – Club Member Edward C.P. "Ned" Edwards elected to U.S. Squash Hall of Fame

2004 – Inaugural Women's Club Open Singles Championship won by Ann E. McGowan

2007 – Club Member Kenton Jernigan elected to U.S. Squash Hall of Fame

2008 – Inaugural Century National Doubles Championships (hosted annually since)

2008 – Inaugural Women's Open Doubles Championship won by Elizabeth W. Del Deuca and Elizabeth "Lee" Belknap

2011 – Hosts World Doubles Championships won by Head Professional Damien Mudge (also hosted in 2013 and won by Damien Mudge)

UNIVERSITY CLUB MEMBERS'
U.S. NATIONAL SQUASH TITLES

Name	Title	Year(s)
Singles		
Beekman H. Pool (Harvard)	Collegiate Champion	1932
Beekman H. Pool	National Singles	1932, '33
Edward C.P. "Ned" Edwards (Penn)	Collegiate Champion	1982
Kenton Jernigan (Harvard)	Collegiate Champion	1983, '84, '86
Kenton Jernigan	National Singles	1983, '84, '85, '92
Frank J. "Jeff" Stanley IV (Princeton)	Collegiate Champion	1987, '88
Frank J. "Jeff" Stanley IV	National Singles	1987
Libby Eynon Welch (Harvard)	Collegiate Champion	1995
Kenton Jernigan	National 40+ Singles	2005
Bruce S. Brickman	National 60+ Singles	2013
Doubles		
Ramsey W. Vehslage III	North American Open Doubles	1966, '67
James A. Dean (Yale)	Intercollegiate Doubles	1992, '93, '94
Edward C. P. "Ned" Edwards	North American Open Doubles	1989, '90, '91
Kenton Jernigan	North American Open Doubles	1993
Frank J. "Jeff" Stanley IV	North American Open Doubles	1995
Jess Berline (Franklin & Marshall)	Intercollegiate Doubles	1997
William P. Osnato (Princeton)	Intercollegiate Doubles	2003
Ryan F. O'Connell	National Amateur Doubles	2005
Garnet S. Booth (Harvard)	Intercollegiate Doubles	2006
John M. Conway	40+ Doubles	2006
Zachary Linhart (Bowdoin)	Intercollegiate Doubles	2007
James M. McLain	Father–Son Century Doubles	2008
Thomas A. Clayton	40+ Doubles	2008, '09
Christopher W. D. "Kip" Gould	Mixed Century Doubles	2008, '11
James M. McLain	Century Legend Doubles	2008
Robert S. Gibralter	Century "A" Doubles	2008
Marc Devorsetz	Century "A" Doubles	2009
Edward C.P. "Ned" Edwards	Century Open Doubles	2009
Theodore R. Marmor	70+ Doubles	2010, '11
Frank J. "Jeff" Stanley IV	Century Open Doubles	2010
Ryan F. O'Connell	Century Legends Doubles	2010
Kenneth C. Leung	Century Legends Doubles	2010
James D. Marver	Century "A" Doubles	2010
Emily Ash Lungtrum	National Open Mixed	2011
Aaron Zimmerman	Century Master Doubles	2013
Libby E. Welch	Century Mixed Doubles	2013
Ann E. McGowan	Century Women's Doubles	2014
William A. Ullman	50+ Doubles	2014
Jerome P. Cortellesi	80+ Doubles	2014

IX

FITNESS

by Philip R. Sprayregen

Since the opening of the clubhouse in 1899, the Gentleman's Bathing Establishment, as it was then known, has been an integral part of the Club's socializing and activity. Over the past 115 years, the nature of activity has metamorphosed considerably. Nonetheless, McKim's noble Classic Italian Renaissance design is intact.

From 1899 well into the 1960s, the Bathing Establishment was oriented more to leisure than exercise. Referring to it as anything other than a bathing facility would be a misnomer. Activities had no semblance of what we currently consider fitness and exercise. The original version had the grand swimming pool as its centerpiece, adjacent were the sauna, steam rooms and massage area. A typical day at the Bathing Department would start with a visit to the steam or hot room, followed by a "plunge" in the pool, concluding with a massage. There were five full-time and two part-time masseurs. Full bar service was offered in the main changing area, and smoking was commonplace. For years, the popular "health" drink was Scotch & milk punch. What is now the aerobic exercise area contained beds, complete with linens. Many members finished their visit by taking an afternoon nap. This lasted for about eighty years.

The 1980s ushered in a rise in the popularity of exercise. The focus changed from passive activity to healthy aerobic and anaerobic exercise. Over time, the room with beds was transformed into the aerobic exercise area, complete with machines for running, rowing, cycling and climbing. What had been a closet became a stretching area. Later, a machine room was annexed and is now a weight room. A filtration system was added to the pool, which is used not only for "plunges," but also for swimming laps. The steam and sauna have been upgraded, but the original design remains. A whirlpool tub was added in the 1980s, and the Fitness Center hired full-time and part-time employees, who hold various degrees in phys-ed & physiology. Yoga, core training, personal training, as well as other disciplines are offered. Though there is no bar service and smoking is strictly prohibited, one can still get a massage.

Since women have been admitted as University Club members, the Fitness Center Committee has endeavored to provide them with meaningful athletic facilities, so they, too, can participate in exercise and sporting activities such as squash. The current women's facilities are located on the eleventh floor, above the squash courts and men's lockers. The women's locker room is shared by fitness members and squash players. With the recent approval of a major construction project on the roof of the clubhouse, exercise and locker facilities will be enlarged and updated to accommodate the expanding female membership.

Top: Locker room, Ladies' Fitness Center
Bottom: Ladies' Fitness Center

Top: Stretching Room, Men's Fitness Center
Bottom: Lounge, Men's Fitness Center

X

THE CLUB TODAY

MUSIC

by Michael L. Royce

Inaugurated in 1947, the Musical Affairs Committee provides ongoing musical performances, salons, activities and educational opportunities for the enjoyment of Club members. Carefully determined by Committee members with extensive knowledge and experience in the world of music, the selected programs encompass many musical genres, including, but not limited to, instrumental and vocal recitals, symphony orchestras, chamber music, opera, dance, jazz, cabaret, folk, experimental, glee concerts and early compositions.

Members have been fortunate to observe a plethora of events—once-in-a-lifetime performances at the Club with internationally known musicians and singers such as Itzhak Perlman and Beverly Sills—which have proven to be so popular they become annual events members rely on and anticipate with delight and enthusiasm.

In some cases, the Committee will advocate for and implement a program that takes place outside of the clubhouse to showcase something special, such as invigorating outings at the Brooklyn Academy of Music, Lincoln Center, the Joyce Theater, the New York Philharmonic, the Metropolitan Opera House, City Center, and the American Ballet Theater, to name a few.

One does not find it surprising that music is so popular with members of the Club. It always has been. One of the Club's founding members, Henry Holt,

attributes music as part of his core education at the St. Timothy School, where he played the organ. Further, in his autobiography, *Garrulities of an Octogenarian Editor*, Holt states that music was very much a part of his life at Yale University, where he was solo first-bass in the choir. And, he was not alone. One of the original thirteen incorporators of the Club, George T. Strong, served on the Board of the New York Philharmonic.

Music not only played a part in the lives of the men who created the Club, but it is also visibly linked to the architects McKim, Mead & White. Researchers will find in the collection of papers once owned by and dear to William Rutherford Mead, along with personal photographs, letters, and other important aspects of his life, several dozen music scores.

With this rich history, bringing music in all of its forms to the Club is a privilege, and the Committee's care and deliberation over what is presented speaks to that privilege. Though music can be defined simply as an art form whose medium is sound and silence, the complexities of experiencing it are infinite. The word "music" is derived from the Greek's use of *mousike*, which means the "art of the Muses," and indeed music inspires and sometimes transforms our spirits. It is an ancient form of human expression that is as relevant today as it was thousands of years ago, when Neanderthals would carve four holes into a juvenile cave bear femur bone to make sound. The Committee hopes that music will always play an important part in the Club—today, tomorrow, and throughout the next 150 years.

BRIDGE   *by David O. Beim*

During the 19th century, whist[1] was the most popular card game in America. Although we have no records so far back, we can be sure that playing whist was a highly popular activity in early days at The University Club. Indeed, New York City's The Regency Whist Club (formerly the Whist Club) was founded for the express purpose of playing the game. Around the turn of the century, whist evolved into auction bridge,

Play was quite gentlemanly, although two club champions in the 1970s...often quarreled loudly and ferociously over finer points of the game.

and in the 1920s, this was replaced by contract bridge, the modern game. By the 1950s, contract bridge had become enormously popular among people of all ages— working adults, school kids, everyone.

The Club's "Card Room Activities" during the 1952–53 season consisted of twenty-six bridge tournaments of various kinds. Most of these were played in College Hall and lasted from 5:30 p.m. to 11:00 p.m., with a one-hour break for dinner, though three were inter-club tournaments played in the Union League Club, the Manhattan Club and the Whist Club.

Some of the twenty-six tournaments were among teams consisting of members and outside guests. In one competition, teams represented graduates of the same university; in one, they represented members of the same college fraternity; in another, they represented "university clubs" from various cities. The huge popularity of bridge was reflected in the imaginative diversity of these events.

Only one tournament in 1952–53 was a mixed pair game for members and ladies. The popularity of mixed pair events grew over time, however, and by the 1970s, there were numerous mixed pair evenings that were elegant, black-tie events. After women were finally admitted to membership in 1987, all games included women. At the first of these, two women showed up and at the beginning of play, the self-conscious men all stood and introduced themselves.

The Club first offered bridge lessons in January-March 1954, when two of the greatest players of the day, ACBL President Peter Leventritt and three-time world champion John Crawford, offered lessons on alternating weeks for $1.50 per person (an overnight room at the Club then cost $6-9).

Card Room - circa 1903

Augie Boehm - Teaching Bridge

---

[1] Like modern bridge, but with neither auction nor dummy.

The Tap Room existed in those days, but a sub-bar was located on the fourth floor and catered to informal games in the Card Room from 4 p.m. on daily, presided over for half a century by the faithful barman George. Play was quite gentlemanly, although two Club champions in the 1970s, Dr. Robert Tater and Dr. James Ducey, often quarreled loudly and ferociously over finer points of the game.

United States national bridge champion August Boehm has had a long association with The University Club, and in the 1970s, he recruited three other bridge celebrities (Sam Stayman, Edgar Kaplan, and Alan Truscott) to give a series of two-hour bridge classes that periodically filled College Hall over five or six years.

On April 17, 1981, Alan Truscott featured a hand from one of the mixed pairs evenings in his *New York Times* bridge column. He noted, "The 'winners' were Dr. Douglas Torre and August Boehm, but they were disqualified, giving the victory to Mr. & Mrs. Joseph Broadus. The event was for mixed partnerships, and neither of the 'winners' had taken the trouble to don an appropriate disguise."

Since the 1980s, the Club has settled into a schedule of one Club tournament per month and one inter-club game per month. The NY Inter-Club Bridge League, founded in 1933, is probably the world's oldest continuously operating bridge organization. Ten clubs, including ours, are members. We generally send two teams, i.e., eight players, to their monthly games. While most other clubs send the same players each time (their champions), we have tended to rotate our teams among numerous interested members, to give more people the chance to participate. Peter and Anne-Marie Embiricos have been Club bridge champions in recent years, and Peter currently heads the Inter-Club Bridge League.

Augie Boehm has continued his long and loyal association with us, giving intermediate bridge lessons once a week on Monday evenings from 6 to 8 p.m. In recent years, he has been joined by Sam Guzzardo, the individual Inter-Club bridge champion in the 1990s, who gives beginning-level lessons at the same time. These lessons provide a wonderful pathway for those taking up this endlessly fascinating game.

BILLIARDS

by Jerome P. Cortellesi

In the Club's early history—in fact up until the late 1930s—billiards figured very prominently and was generally considered by many to be the social center of the Club. At 9 Brevoort Place—the Club's first home (1865–67)—billiards was enjoyed, although it is suspected that there was but a single table.

At the second home at Fifth Avenue and 35th Street (1879–84), space was shared on the second floor with the incipient Library.

However, when the Club relocated to the Leonard Jerome mansion at Madison Avenue and 26th Street, the sport took on added dimensions. At this stately edifice, the three billiard and two pool tables were positioned on the first floor.

One of the reasons for considering the construction of the new home at Fifth Avenue and 54th Street was the promise of even larger and more elegant billiard quarters. Indeed, seven tables, along with four attendants, were installed upstairs in a mezzanine area that in later years became the Tap Room. Given the importance attached to this fine pastime, many of the members were disappointed with this out-of-the-way location. In fact, a serious—but failed—attempt was mounted to find an alternative ground floor site. But despite these protests, it remained on the second floor until 1918, when the space of what is now College Hall was created, largely to accommodate expanded billiard activity. There, now with twelve tables, billiards and pool remained very much at the center of attention. Befitting its location, a professional instructor (Mr. B. Slater) was engaged as manager of the facilities.

In 1938, with enthusiasm declining, then President Walter Hope and others had designs on the billiard room. In a "bold stroke," without consulting the membership, all of the tables were "temporarily" removed to accommodate a "Horse and Buggy Days Party" on election night, November 8, 1938. The announcement read that "the room was made available that evening through the courtesy of the Billiard Committee." The Committee was misled, to say the least. Billiards never returned to the future College Hall.

Members at the annual Billiard Committee dinner

What later became the Grill Room was the next home. All was downsized to five tables—three billiard and two pool tables. As participation continued to decline, in 1947, much-diminished quarters were established on the fifth floor, with one billiard and just two pool tables. It remained there until Jerome Cortellesi became Chairman of the Billiards Committee in 1989. With the intention to revitalize billiards participation, a series of promotional events was developed which re-

sulted in a renewed interest in the sport. Accordingly, it became apparent that a larger, more practical venue was needed. Presentations were made to the House Committee suggesting a return to the Grill Room (which could be closed, resulting in a considerable expense reduction at no service inconvenience to the membership). This was accepted and billiards was now again in splendid quarters, well placed (next to the Tap Room) with four tables—one billiard and three pool tables.

Over the years, a number of prominent personalities have taken an active interest in the sport. Edgar Appleby, a longtime Chairman of the Billiard Committee, was several times a National Amateur Champion. Leo Welch, Chairman of Exxon Corp., played regularly, as did Judge Harold R. Medina (for whom the annual Medina Cup is named).

A renewed interest in billiards (for the most part encompassing the various games of pool) is very much in evidence these days, under the able guidance of the current chairman, Thomas W. Brown. Annual championship matches are held for Eight Ball, Cowboy, Nine Ball, Straight (14.1) Pool and, of course, billiards. The Club also participates in various interclub contests within the city.

BACKGAMMON & CHESS

by Matthew H. Ahrens

Backgammon and chess have been popular social activities at the Club throughout our 150-year history, and the Club has provided for a broad range of special events, tournaments and social parties. Among the world's oldest board games, each requires a high level of analysis and strategy as each player elects tactics by assessing options and opponents' possible counter-moves. The academic nature of the Club's membership makes both games a natural fit.

Backgammon, in particular, has played a special role, since it provides a forum to get together with old friends, make new ones, drink a little too much, and all over a game which combines the best of chess, poker, and Lady Luck.

Throughout the years, backgammon rooms with tables available for use—and frequently used—have been set up in various parts of the clubhouse, including the Dwight Lounge, the Card Room and the men's squash locker room. The area known as the Backgammon Alcove in the Tap Room currently has five tables permanently available and has become backgammon's primary home at the Club. In recent years, members roll dice in the Alcove nearly every weekday afternoon and evening.

In addition, since at least the 1950s, the Club has hosted monthly backgammon dinners. Since the 1990s, every dinner has had a "theme," ranging from Steak Backgammon Dinners to Mardi Gras Backgammon to August in Provence to Bond and Backgammon to annual Black Tie Awards dinners. Recently, summer members have been active participants; attendance in the summer months can exceed 100 players!

The Club has also held an annual singles backgammon tournament since 1904, an annual handicap backgammon tournament since 1988, and an annual summer doubles backgammon tournament since 1989. Annual interclub tournaments are currently being held with the Union Club and London's Royal Automobile Club, and there have been prior tournaments with other clubs, including the New York Athletic Club. Trophies are awarded to tournament winners, and tournament cups have been on display in a trophy case in the Alcove. Somehow, the singles tournament cup was "misplaced" in the late 1970s/early 1980s, and the names of the tournament winners between 1904 and 1972 were "lost in antiquity."

Chess once had an important place in the life of the Club, as evidenced by the several sets of carved ivory pieces on display on the fourth floor, but has fallen into desuetude. In 1923, for example, the second game of the U.S. Chess Championship, between Frank T. Marshall and Edward Lasker, was played at the Club. The chessboard and pieces on display in the Douglas Reading Room were once used by Garry Kasparov, and were a gift to the Club. Interest in chess has risen and fallen over the years, and tournaments may have been held at times. Chessboards have often been set in areas ranging from the Dwight Lounge in the 1930s to the Conversation Room on the Library floor.

WINE   *by James K. Finkel*

The University Club's first known Wine and Food Dinner was held in March 1936 and was suggested by the Entertainment Committee. Members were invited to come in "Full Dress"—guests not permitted—and were requested not to have cocktails before the event, nor to smoke during. In the same tradition as we have today, the dinner began in the Breakfast Room with aperitifs and hors d'oeuvres. The limit was 125 guests and it appears that 118 were present.

Ernest Peixotto spoke regarding the wines and provided the illustration on the menu of "The Bacchic Pilgrimage." Prominent attorney Henry W. Taft was the head of the Food and Wine Society at the time. The menu and wine pairings would be considered unusual, but not uninteresting, today. This event was replicated in March 2015 in celebration of the Sesquicentennial. The menu:

- Braised Celeri à la Watch Hill Farm, followed by Fromage Stilton, served with Corton Charlemagne 1929

- Pintade Supreme, served with Grand Chambertin 1911
- Saumon Fumé de la Nouvelle Ecosse, Petite Marmite Okra and Homard Supreme, served with Montilla Tio Frasquito + Amontillado Imperial Sherries
- Rocher de Glace Manhattan aux Amandes, served with Lanson Vintage 1923 and Moet & Chandon Vintage 1926 Champagnes
- Café Noir, served with an Otard Cognac VSOP

The origins of the Wine Committee undoubtedly stem from the Wine and Food Society; however, the precise timing of its creation and standing as an Informal Committee are unknown.

The Wine Committee's work has, by necessity, always been coordinated with Club management, and in recent years, the dedicated Purchasing Managers have been Ken Symons (1983–1998) and Michael Trager (1999–present). As well, assistance with dinner planning and execution has been provided by John Grieco (2013–present). And our Club's General Manager, John Dorman, has officiated at several industry wine competitions, as well as instituted a sommelier program for weeknights in the Main Dining Room.

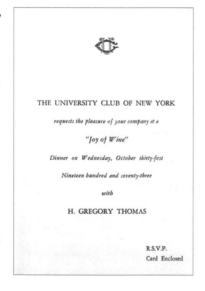

THE UNIVERSITY CLUB OF NEW YORK

requests the pleasure of your company at a

"Joy of Wine"

Dinner on Wednesday, October thirty-first

Nineteen hundred and seventy-three

with

H. GREGORY THOMAS

R.S.V.P.
Card Enclosed

One helpful record is the invitation to the first Joy of Wine Dinner in 1973. That event was presided over by member H. Gregory Thomas, a noted oenophile who was photographed in his robe as Grand Maître de la Commanderie de Bordeaux (thus, he was the U.S. national head of the leading Bordeaux society).

Much can be said of each of the past Chairs of the Wine Committee, but allowing for his extended term, we see that H. Gregory Thomas was a "larger than life" figure (his stature accompanied by his commanding height). He was an erudite Southern gentleman, who was known in the realm of wine to "not suffer fools gladly." Reminiscences of Thomas include his encyclopedic memory, and his habit of spontaneously challenging those around him to describe wines in detail. He bequeathed his collection of wine books to the Club Library, as well.

The Wine Committee's efforts over the years have dramatically improved our wine program and continue to maintain the reputation of The University Club as having one of the preeminent cellars and high quality member service in the country, if not the world. The Club owes this in large part to prior chairmen and committee members, as it continues to enjoy great bottles purchased years ago. Despite a massive increase in wine prices over the past ten to fifteen years, the Wine Committee has continued the primary mission to purchase and offer great value wines to members.

The Wine Committee has continued the longstanding traditions of the Joy of Wine Dinner (held every November)—a celebration of some of the grand cru wines from the cellars, and the Game Dinner (held in January/February), which seeks to pair bolder wines with seasonal wild game cuisine. In 2009, Chairman James Finkel began a new tradition with an annual historic wine personality dinner: featured notables have been Napoleon, Thomas Jefferson, Winston Churchill, Alfred Hitchcock, Charles Dickens, and Julius Caesar. In 2010, another tradition began with an annual educational tasting and dinner led by Clive Coates, MW.

It may be said that the Wine Committee's large focus in expanding the Club's wine holdings, until the mid-1990s, was on the wines of Bordeaux, with some attention to Italian, Californian and German wines. Under the leadership of Doug Barzelay, initiatives to acquire more wine from Burgundy began, and were carried forward by the successive Wine Committee chairs. Much credit is owed to Basil Williams for expanding the Wine Committee's ability to deepen the cellar with significant purchases of good vintages.

Under Finkel, the breadth of the Wine Committee's work has both expanded, and yet been somewhat decentralized. In the past, the Chair would select virtually all the wines for the monthly blind tasting, and the Committee members would choose the best wines among them as recommendations to the Club Manager for purchase.

In the past few years, Wine Committee members have been assigned specific regions and appellations, attending trade tastings when possible in their respective realms. Further, each Wine Committee member is charged with the responsibility of co-hosting one of the annual wine dinners, helping select the wines to be served, as well as the food pairings. These responsibilities have allowed the Wine Committee Chair to develop additional events, and also allow for necessary leadership experience to other Committee members.

As Club membership interest in wine has grown, the Wine Committee has expanded the wine by the glass and a half-bottle program in the Tap Room. Wine storage capacity for each of the dining rooms has been improved. The Club's sommeliers have been, in succession, Whitney Woodham, Meredith Wilford, and since 2013, Yannick Benjamin. The format of the wine list has been revised, as well, to accommodate a greater number of selections available to members, as well as being better organized.

The Club has the unusual benefit of a large underground wine cellar, which allegedly was the site of the morgue when St. Luke's Hospital occupied this site. The cellar is comprised of several rooms, all of which are temperature controlled, but are far more industrial looking than what one would expect in the cellars of a great château. Temperature and humidity sensors have been installed, measuring fluctuations which are sought to be remedied, so that the valuable treasures (approximately 25,000 bottles) age under optimal conditions. It is all of this focus and advancement that will allow the Wine Committee to help supply members with high quality libations for many decades to come!

YOUNGER MEMBERS

by R. Fletcher Hall and William S. Simonton II

The Younger Members Committee, formerly the Young Men's Committee, is a twenty-member representation of the members thirty-two years of age or younger to the Club and its formal and informal committees.

The YMC is charged with vetting younger candidates in the admissions process, thus helping provide peer insight on young people vying for University Club membership. This is core to the Committee's responsibilities and one they take with the utmost diligence.

As outreach to other committees is important within our McKim, Mead & White walls, it is important to the surrounding community, as well.

In addition, in recent years, the Younger Members Committee has focused on outreach and leadership development of the younger membership. Committee members are encouraged to reach out to other standing and informal committees of the Club, and serve as ambassadors of the YMC. This enhanced cross-committee communication builds deeper coordination, and brings exciting events to the Club constituency—whether young or old.

Besides cultivating young leadership for further posts, the YMC has had meaningful impact on planning and improving events throughout the Club. The Committee takes great care in electing a Chairperson (or in some instances complete subcommittees) to assist in the planning, organization, and promotion of an event. For many of the Club's younger members, events such as the annual Halloween Dinner Dance and Casino Night were their very first introductions to The University Club as guests. Both events sell out months in advance and continue to be staples among the Club's special evenings. Furthermore, each year, the Committee continues to work toward adding additional events to the calendar. In 2012, the Committee introduced the "Annual Young Member Ping Pong Night" to great fanfare, and in 2014 worked with the Billiards Committee to introduce a "Billiards and Brew" night in the Tap Room.

As outreach to other committees is important within our McKim, Mead & White walls, it is important to the surrounding community, as well. Each year, the YMC sponsors an event in conjunction with the Big Apple Circus and the Children's Aid Society to provide Circus tickets to underprivileged children in the five boroughs of New York City. With the Club venturing into its 150th year—and many more on the way—it is important to note that it has had such a glorious and long run due to the commitment of new and younger members. Thusly, the Younger Members Committee's role remains essential to the backbone of the Club, to make sure we can celebrate another 150 years with future youthful members' support.

SPECIAL EVENTS

by Barbara A. Taylor

The Special Events Committee began in 1994 as the Senior Events Committee, an initiative spearheaded by a group of retired members. The variety and success of the initial programs motivated the Committee to attract the general body of members, and the name was changed to Special Events Committee. The Committee's mission is to provide unique experiences that match the wide variety of interests of Club members. Each event is designed to have a "special" quality, such as providing a feature or aspect that is not available to the general public.

The selection of events represents some of the most educational, entertaining and cultural attractions available, keeping in mind the need for choices at different times of day, so that all members have the opportunity to participate.

The number of events offered by the Committee has grown substantially over the years, starting from six in year one to an average of more than fifty for each year since 2010. Many of the events are instructional programs that take place inside the clubhouse. These events feature access to highly talented experts in various areas and the opportunities to get to know other Club members. Members are able to enjoy small group language lessons (Italian, French and Spanish), and learn more about a variety of culinary treats and beverages through seminars and tastings orchestrated by experts on topics including caviar, chocolate, the civilization of beer, and a popular ongoing series of classes on fine wines from different regions. Numerous sessions are led by knowledgeable professionals in areas such as the American Academy in Rome, Hemingway in Cuba and Key West, and America's Gilded Age. A selection of interactive educational programs provides useful tips on topics ranging from social media to jewelry and photography. Events repeated each year that feature evening entertainment include movie screenings and themed dances.

In 2012, the Committee introduced a series of monthly roundtable salon events on timely topics like issues in the Middle East with the former head of Saudi Intelligence, and defense in America with a former member of the Joint Chiefs of Staff. These small group discussions led by highly knowledgeable experts became an ongoing program.

In recent years, the Committee has hosted the "Salute to Our Armed Services" luncheon to honor a group of active-duty members of the Navy, Marines and Coast Guard who are in New York City for Fleet Week. Club members visit with members of our armed services face-to-face and thank them for their service to our country.

The Special Events program also offers members a host of activities outside the Club in metropolitan New York and nearby states. Escorted visits exclusively for Club members and their guests to a variety of local museums have been a popular tradition since 1994.

Club members in India, 2008

These include the Museum of Modern Art, the Metropolitan Museum of Art, the Frick Collection and the Whitney Museum, among others, and often take place when the museums are closed to the general public. Members also have opportunities to experience Broadway and off-Broadway theatre productions, concerts and sports events.

As a result of members' interest in learning more about the boroughs of New York City, an ongoing series of escorted walking tours started in 2012. Recent tours have featured highlights of Harlem, the downtown area, and Williamsburg, Brooklyn. Local offerings also feature visits to attractions like the Brooklyn Botanical Garden during the peak of cherry blossom season, the New York Botanical Garden for the Monet exhibition and the annual Orchid Show, the *Intrepid* during Fleet Week, the High Line, the Coast Guard Station in Staten Island and the 9/11 Memorial.

Half- or full-day bus trips take members to sites beyond the New York metropolitan area. Highlights have been the Barnes Foundation's art collection in Philadelphia and visits to Old Westbury Gardens, Winterthur, Tuxedo Park, and Kykuit, the Rockefeller estate.

A program of annual international tours appeals to members' interest in traveling with one another. Recently, small groups have taken escorted trips to Greece and Turkey, India, Japan and South Africa.

ANNUAL EVENTS

by Edward A. Reilly Jr.

As with many committees, what goes on within the walls of One West 54th Street is of the utmost importance. However, a close second is making sure the Club members enjoy singular moments outside these walls, as well. The Special Events Committee prides itself on succeeding at both.

The University Club's Annual Events Committee consists of thirteen members who represent a diverse mix of people. The Committee members offer perspectives of different ages, genders, and interests and contribute to a wide variety of happenings. Ranging from the 2014 Thanksgiving brunch event, which was attended by nearly one thousand members and guests, to an Etiquette Class attended by thirty children between the ages of seven and thirteen, the annual events span a wide swath of interests.

These offerings have not always been so robust. The Committee was initially formed in 1959. Over the years as the Club has grown with the admission of women as members and the acceptance of children at many happenings, the Committee has responded to these changes and added numerous events and expanded and updated the format of many others to adapt to the changing demographics of the Club and the interests of the members. It is noteworthy that, while many of the Club's committees have a specific focus, the Annual Events Committee's mandate is to create and steward offerings that appeal to the full range of interests of the Club's members.

Many of the Committee's events are traditional ones, such as the Valentine's Day, Christmas and New Year's Eve Dinner Dances, Easter, Mother's Day and Thanksgiving brunches, the Family Night Dinner, the New Year's Day buffet, the Club's Annual Meeting, the Senior Members Night, the Committee Appreciation Dinner and the 25 Year Club Dinner. The Committee works to keep these events fresh and running smoothly by offering suggestions on the food and the format. The Committee is at its finest, however, when it creates new or overhauled events that add to the Club's vitality and appeal to different elements of the Club's membership.

The introduction of the Easter Bunny at the Easter brunch and Santa at the Family Night Dinner are examples of how the Committee has enhanced events to broaden their appeal and attract families with kids. The etiquette class has been a great event welcomed by children and parents alike. The annual Mother Daughter Tea has a broad appeal, often bringing three generations together at the Club. The children's Gingerbread Workshop has attracted families to the Club to celebrate the holidays and has proven to be an enormous success, with over two hundred children and their parents decorating gingerbread houses in the Main Dining Room.

One of Percy Douglas' aspirations for the Club was that it hold a debate between teams from prominent universities each year. The Annual Events Committee took on the task of effecting that aspiration and now hosts the annual Percy Douglas Debate each year in November. In 2013, the tenth year of the debate, a team of debaters representing Johns Hopkins, Columbia and Harvard debated a team from West Point in a lively exchange over affirmative action. In previous years, teams representing Princeton, Smith, USMA, Fordham, NYU, MIT, Penn and Columbia have participated in the debate. The Percy Douglas Debate trophy is on display in the Tap Room.

Each year in January, the Committee collaborates with the American Scottish Foundation to present Burns Night, a celebration of Scottish culture featuring Scotch whiskies, traditional Scottish music and Scottish fare, of course including haggis. This lively event attracts a mix of Club members and guests from the

Two potential future members enjoying Family Night, 2013

The winning team at the 2013 Percy Douglas Debate

Foundation; 2014 was the nineteenth year for this event. Other cultures are honored through the Annual Events Committee's programs such as the Cinco de Mayo dinner celebrating Mexican independence, the Evening in St. Tropez evoking summer in France, Oktoberfest featuring German cuisine, and the recent addition of a Columbus Day dinner featuring a prominent Italian chef each year.

Many of the Committee's events are designed to be informative, as well as entertaining. In addition to the etiquette class, the Annual Meeting and the debate, each year the Committee presents a tasting of a different spirit, broadening the concept of the traditional Scotch tasting. The tastings feature a talk by a prominent expert on that particular spirit. In 2013, the event was entitled The Art of Japanese Whisky Tasting and featured Japanese drinks and delicacies.

During the summer, the Committee offers several events to appeal to the Club's summer members. These events are an opportunity to introduce the summer members to the Club's social life and gives them an opportunity to mingle with the rest of the membership in a festive environment. The Evening in St. Tropez, which features summery French cuisine and evokes the feeling of a summer party in the south of France, is one. The other special summer events are the Barbeque Night with a southwestern flair and Lobster Night featuring an enhanced buffet and especially large Maine lobsters.

Though every event is important, New Year's Eve is perhaps the Committee's signature. This black tie evening features a new theme each year. In 2013, the theme was a New Year's Eve in Venice featuring gondolas, barber poles and Venetian masks. The festivities typically kick off with a champagne and caviar reception on the first floor of the Club. The main party then moves to the seventh floor for an elegant dinner dance. For those looking for a later start to the evening, Club 54 occupies the Tap Room and features cocktails, an elaborate hors d'oeuvres spread and a disk jockey. At midnight, all of the partyers meet on the seventh floor for a champagne toast and the ball drop. Thereafter, the festivities continue until the wee hours of the morning at Club 54 and for dessert in the Percy Douglas Reading Room.

The Club's 150th anniversary has inspired a new annual event which will celebrate the Club's founding. While the details of the annual Birthday Party are still being worked out, the Annual Events Committee is very enthusiastic about creating another event to honor the Club and entertain the membership on April 28 of each year.

HOUSE COMMITTEE

by Charles T. Locke III

It is safe to say that The University Club is as vibrant today as at any time in its 150-year history and is currently preeminent among New York City's private clubs. When we pass through the front doors of The University Club, we enter an oasis, an atmosphere which is familiar and convivial. Invariably, we are greeted by cheerful and attentive staff as we dine, attend a lecture, play squash, work out in the Fitness Center or simply relax in the Douglas Reading Room or Library and read. And whether we're reserving a single room or scheduling a banquet for 200 guests, the process is seamless. However, behind the scenes is a complex and finely tuned operation which manages the facilities and provides the services we've come to cherish, all under the direct supervision of our General Manager and the oversight of the House Committee. It's the equivalent of simultaneously operating a ninety-seven-room hotel, multiple restaurants, several athletic and fitness facilities, and a world-class library. Did you know, for example, that in 2013, the Club served 85,000 à la carte meals, hosted 1,397 member-sponsored events, held 213 Club functions attended by a total of approximately 20,000 members and guests, and provided 22,400 rooms to overnight members and sponsored guests? Crucial to the success of the Club are the 275 dedicated employees who ensure that member services are available at all times, even during unusual and debilitating circumstances like the power outage of 2003, the transit strike of 2005 or extreme weather conditions such as Hurricane Sandy in 2012 or the winter of 2013–2014.

Ultimate oversight of the Club's affairs rests with the Council and, for specific areas of responsibility, the various standing committees of the Club. However, few of these committees are as involved in every facet of managing the Club's operation as the House Committee. From the mundane ("too much salt in my soup") to the macro (the College Hall construction project), the House Committee has been involved.

Comprised of no more than ten members who meet monthly, with the President and Treasurer in attendance, the House Committee's sweeping duties, as stated in the Constitution, include: i) supervising management of the Club, ii) reviewing and delegating authority for day-to-day operations to the Club's General Manager, iii) regulating prices, iv) establishing and enforcing the Club's House Rules, v) reviewing and setting policy for Club and member-sponsored events and activities, vi) addressing deportment and disciplinary issues involving members and guests, vii) receiving complaints and redressing grievances, viii) recommending reciprocal club arrangements to the Council, ix) consulting with the Capital Planning and Finance Committees on receipt and expense budgets, capital budgets and forecasts, and x) such other similar duties as the Council may assign to it.

Over the years, the House Committee has responded to a constantly changing economic and social environment. Before, during and after the financial crisis in 2008, the Committee evaluated the effects of the economy and demographics upon the membership and made appropriate changes in the members' dues, entrance fees, and summer guest fees, while continually assessing the impact of the economy on a $30+ million annual budget. In 2009, the Club completed the sale of excess development rights (air rights) to the Museum of Modern Art. In deliberation with other committees, the House Committee was involved in the recommendations regarding the investment and use of the proceeds of the sale. Incidental to the sale was the major restoration/renovation of the main entrance of the Club, as required by the Landmark Preservation Commission.

The House Committee continues to have a presence and frequently collaborates with the Capital Planning Committee. However, prior to formation of a formal Capital Planning Committee in 2007, the House Committee was even more deeply involved in the construction projects in the clubhouse. The Committee devoted substantial time and effort to projects, which included the renovation of the men's fitness center, installation of the women's fitness center, the transformation of the squash facilities from American courts to International courts, as well as many other improvements. The House Committee is also attuned to societal changes while protecting the traditional ambiance of the Club. It initiated a members' survey in 2013, analyzed the responses and, as a result, made various recommendations, including modest revisions to the House Rules regarding the dress code and the use of cellphones and electronic readers.

The House Committee has also been instrumental over recent years in establishing reciprocal relationships with highly esteemed private clubs in London, Paris, Rome, Florence, Madrid, Hong Kong, Buenos Aires, and elsewhere. Enjoyment of those facilities has proven to be a valuable benefit for our members.

Each year, the House Committee's efforts have been focused on the budget and the monthly financial results, with special emphasis on the primary drivers, namely, dues/entrance fees, payroll and benefits, food and beverage, rooms and administrative and general expenses. These efforts, in collaboration with the other committees, the Council and the Club's management, have paid

dividends and share credit for The University Club's outstanding success. The Club is financially sound, the clubhouse infrastructure is in excellent condition, there is a wait list for new members, and member satisfaction with the services is extremely high, as evidenced by the recent survey results.

The University Club has seen many changes over the past decades, and the House Committee's agenda has varied widely, involving issues which the Club's founders could never have imagined. One can only wonder what issues will confront the Committee 150 years from now.

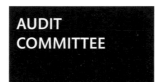

AUDIT COMMITTEE

by Martin L. Budd

As its name implies, the Audit Committee, through its long existence, has had an important but not very exciting role in the governance of the Club. Its primary role is and has been to interface on behalf of the Club with the Club's independent accountants. However, in recent times, the ever-growing complexity of the financial, tax and accounting worlds has made the issues with which the Committee has to deal significantly more interesting.

For example, keeping an eye on how much revenue the Club earns from non-members is a recurring and crucial role. If the Club receives too much revenue from non-members, it could become a fully taxable entity under IRS rules. The Club's recent multimillion dollar sale of its air rights to the Museum of Modern Art required compliance with a complex set of IRS rules over a substantial period of time to ensure that the proceeds of the sale were not fully taxable. As one would expect, the Committee monitored compliance carefully. Another example of modern complexity is the fact that the Club's unionized employees belong to pension plans which include as beneficiaries other members of the union who work for other clubs, and therefore, the Club is jointly liable with the other clubs for the benefits due under these multi-employer pension plans. Accordingly, the Club could have significant unexpected liabilities if one of the other employers fails or the assets of the multi-employer plans fall materially below the financial obligations of the plans. The Committee watches these issues carefully to ensure that the Club is not confronted with any unpleasant surprises. In all of these matters, the Committee works closely with our outstanding management, obtaining and monitoring the relevant facts and taking action where necessary.

Finally, the Committee has been spending more time brainstorming the possible new risks to the Club which may accompany the use of new technologies. As a result, the Audit Committee, in conjunction with the House Committee, has worked with our insurance advisors to obtain significant insurance to cover possible breaches of our computer data.

Thus, not surprisingly, the subjects to which the Audit Committee must pay attention have changed significantly over recent years, reflecting how the world as a whole has changed. Nevertheless, the devotion to the Club's members remains as strong as ever.

FINANCE COMMITTEE
by Warren H. Haber

The past seven years have been particularly transformative and financially beneficial for the Club, given the sale of the development rights to the Museum of Modern Art on December 15, 2009. Since that time, there have been a number of physical enhancements to our historic structure, exemplary of which is the new front entrance, consistent with the Landmark Preservation Commission requisite. There have also been a number

of infrastructure and interior renovations, including the detailed restoration of the Library, guest room renovations, and heating and air conditioning upgrades, to name a few. These capital projects have magnified both the importance of having engaged participant members serve on our Committee and the need for consistent financial oversight given the Constitutional mandate: to supervise the finances and investments of the Club and the investments of the Club's retirement plans. Given that the Club presently has substantial invested capital, the Finance Committee has formed three informal subcommittees to oversee specific segments of the Club's investment portfolio and arrange for both periodic on-site meetings, at the designated asset managers' facilities, and quarterly meetings of the investment managers' firms with the entire Finance Committee at the Club. At these meetings, discussions are held regarding overall market conditions, current thinking and prospects in light of these conditions and the potential asset class reallocation. All of these issues are evaluated in light of the Club's annual budget, five-year forecast, and future capital expenditure programs.

Annually, the Finance Committee is charged with presenting a fiscal year receipt and expenses budget to the Executive Committee. Given the recent College Hall enhancement project, members of House, Capital Planning and Finance, along with the Treasurer, have met more frequently to review the revenue trends, expenses and particularly capital expenditures, both normalized ongoing capital expenditures and specific future projects. Funding sources and financing alternatives are also reviewed and discussed at these subcommittee meetings.

The other significant annual constitutional initiative assigned to the Finance Committee, in consultation with the Capital Planning and House Committees, is the annual preparation of a five-year forecast of receipts and expenses, along with capital expenditures for the same period. Specific projects are reviewed and prioritized for the period. Funding sources for the capital expenditures are also identified and delineated.

In summary, all of our efforts are to effectively oversee the finances of our esteemed Club, so as to assist and advise the Club management to continue to provide outstanding service to the members and guests, while providing compensation and benefits to dedicated employees. Equally important is to review expenditures so as to continually maintain and enhance one of the architectural masterpieces of our city, that was designed by the highly regarded architectural firm of McKim, Mead & White, and has been the home of The University Club since May 1899.

CAPITAL PLANNING

by Jeffrey Bliss

Removing a balcony at night during the facade restoration.

The two sailors salute the captain. "Sir, we have finished painting the ship, sir!"

"Fine," says the captain, "better get started again ASAP!"

Keeping up with the now 116-year-old clubhouse presents two distinct challenges. We need to maintain the excellence of the building's incomparable physical form, originally made by craftsmen and using practices that are rare or nonexistent today, while at the same time we must often adapt and even change that built form to meet today's and the future needs of the membership.

The Capital Planning Committee is the newest of the Club's standing committees, having been created by an amendment to the constitution in 2006. Previously, construction projects were overseen by an informal planning group consisting of some of the Club's officers and managed by the House Committee chairman. As the scope and complexity of these projects increased

over time, the Council decided that a more formal structure was advantageous.

Capital Planning's present responsibilities pursuant to the constitution are to:

- determine and prioritize the Club's immediate and longer-term capital needs for recommendation to the Council;
- investigate budgeting and financing issues related thereto; and
- plan and supervise projects arising therefrom that are approved for implementation by the Council.

A great deal has been accomplished over the last fifteen years. Among many projects, the major work has included the following:

- In 1999, the Main Reading Room was restored and renamed for former president Percy Douglas, who personally supervised this wonderful project, to celebrate the centenary of the clubhouse.

- From 2001 to 2005 the exterior façades of the clubhouse were completely repaired. This necessary work addressed a great deal of "deferred maintenance," and included the removal and reconstruction of all of the bronze balcony railings and several of the granite balconies themselves, restoration of the masonry throughout, and replacement of virtually all of the 100+-year-old windows with new, double-glazed mahogany sash windows. The Main Dining Room's terrace on the seventh floor was completely redesigned and rebuilt.
- Beginning in 2004 and completed in 2013, all of the Club's guest rooms have been renovated. The Club installed new heating and air conditioning systems to replace antiquated, window-mounted air conditioners, along with new security and environmental control systems and significant upgrades to the furniture and lighting fixtures.
- The Library restoration was a six-year undertaking, begun in 2005, which included installation of air conditioning and climate control systems (for the first time!), an artistic restoration of the Mowbray ceiling murals, the complete repair and refinishing of all woodwork, and the provision of a new sophisticated lighting system throughout.

- Between 2010 and 2013, all clubhouse roofs and skylights were either replaced or restored, and a new terrace for members (to open in 2015) was created on the tenth floor adjacent to the squash doubles court.
- Behind the scenes, significant improvements have been made to the Club's energy and fire protection systems throughout this period, aimed at improving our efficiency and the safety of our members.
- And recently, working with the Landmarks Preservation Commission, the entrance to the clubhouse was transformed, through the installation of a new structural glass canopy and new doors, in order to bring the clubhouse closer to the original intentions of its McKim design.

The principal undertaking of the Committee for 2014 was the implementation of a significant new design for College Hall, along with a complete reconstruction of the kitchen, bathrooms and other necessary infrastructure serving that portion of the ground floor. Intended to coincide with the 150th anniversary of The University Club, this project was originally an initiative of the House Committee, and it took two full years to design and execute.

As ever, Capital Planning continues to work with the other standing committees to assess the needs of the membership and maintain our superb clubhouse.

by David B. Jaffe and Carol Mitchell

While the Club celebrates its founding in the middle of the 19th century, the Non-Resident Committee celebrates its founding at the turn of the 21st!

The present clubhouse serves as an icon of New York architecture, and its location is at the city's cultural heart. However, The University Club itself has never restricted its membership to just local residents. In 1879, the 509 college graduates who were the membership included 87 non-residents. Today, there are about 1,400 non-resident members, almost a third of the total club membership.

The Non-Resident Committee seeks to foster the vital spirit of friendship and engagement that is characteristic of the Club members by arranging events that will introduce far-flung members to each other. Although non-residents come to New York City often, they do not see the clubhouse as merely a hotel, but as an opportunity to connect with others who share their cultural and intellectual visions. The Committee is composed of both resident and non-resident members, with past chairmen hailing from North Carolina and Massachusetts, while the present chairman is from Texas. All have become personal friends because of their connection to The University Club.

Some of the events planned include weekends designated by the Club as "Non-Resident Weekends" allowing the non-residents to meet both each other and resident members. It is firmly believed that there is no better social club in the country than The University Club—namely due to the camaraderie.

We have had dinners in some of the different cities where our non-resident members live, including London, several Florida cities, Charlotte, North Carolina, and Washington, D.C.

At a dinner held at a country club in Miami, two of our members who had not met before were introducing themselves. One asked, "Where do you live?" and the other responded, pointing to the skyline visible through the window, "That tall building over there." Both live in the same building, five floors apart, and now see each other regularly.

That's the power of The University Club.

ADMISSIONS

by Owen P. J. King

The general role of the Committee on Admissions has remained constant since the Club's founding, while the details of its mission and practices have been reinterpreted or altered to reflect changes in both the Club's membership and broader society. Of particular interest is how the Club's distinctive requirement of an undergraduate degree has been understood over the past 150 years and what that has meant for the Committee.

While changes have been made over the years, it should be noted some key points much remain unaltered. The Committee has always remained dedicated to preserving the character of the Club through the review of candidates proposed by members. Since the Club's reorganization in 1879, the Committee has always comprised twenty-one members; two negative votes brings an end to a candidacy; and, perhaps most surprising, the Committee meetings have always been held in the evening of the first Wednesday of each month. Beyond these, much has changed.

At the time of the Club's founding, there was no social institution in the United States that required a college degree for its membership. There had been a number of such clubs and alumni groups formed in Europe, but here in the young republic (still less than one hundred years old), this was a novel—and highly selective—prerequisite. In fact, in 1865, only about 1 percent of American college-age men (and about 0.2 percent of college-age women) were enrolled in institutions of higher education of any type.

The Club further limited the number of those eligible for membership through additional criteria, both social and academic. Not only were the institutions subject to approval by the Club, but also the selectivity extended to the individual degrees at these institutions. The evaluation of the eligibility of degrees focused on three main components: the required course of study for the degree, the period of required residency, and the character of the life and surroundings of the students while pursuing the required studies. These last two points, centered on the quality of the residential experience, became a primary focus across the years in determining qualification for membership.

While the first few decades saw a number of members admitted who had obtained graduate degrees without having first completed undergraduate studies (a common situation for both doctors and lawyers in those days), it was made clear that the required residency at an eligible institution was intended for undergraduate studies specifically. It was further clarified that the quality of residential life was of utmost importance. While there were those who had met the length of residency required while pursuing medicine, theology, or the law, they were not the beneficiaries of the advantages and sympathies fostered by the societies, traditions, sports, and other interests of undergraduate life enjoyed by those pursuing other studies. As such, only those with the necessary undergraduate experience were deemed eligible.

This was just the start of the admissions process, however. Each candidate that had attained an acceptable degree from an acceptable institution then needed to be proposed, seconded, and supported by Club members. Once this was done, the candidate needed to be interviewed by at least four members of the Committee on Admissions. It bears repeating that it takes only two negative votes out of twenty-one Committee members to bring about the end of a candidacy.

These highly subjective and discriminating criteria, along with the proposal and interview processes, had understandable results. By the time the Club moved into the magnificent clubhouse in 1899, more than 70 percent of the membership (roughly 2,400 of the 3,300 members) hailed from just the eleven colleges that today

make up the Ivy League and Little Three. In fact, the eighteen institutions symbolized by the seals on our clubhouse's facades represented nearly 90 percent of the membership at that time.

A special Committee on Colleges and Degrees was created to evaluate colleges and degrees initially on an as-needed basis, eventually becoming a standing committee. Whenever a candidate was proposed who held a degree that was not on the Club's approved list, the degree and institution were investigated by this Committee.

The painstaking and detailed work it performed was impressive, frequently involving ongoing correspondence between the Committee and the president of the institution under review, along with trips to the colleges. The review and input from The University Club helped to create higher and more uniform standards of excellence for American colleges and universities. Indeed, the Club served as an unofficial accreditation organization for many of these institutions. There is even correspondence in the archives between the president of the American Bar Association and some law school presidents expressing his belief that The University Club's evaluation of some law schools would serve to help elevate legal training in America.

While America grew and higher education reached more citizens, the Committee's role remained one more of exclusion than inclusion. By the Club's fiftieth year, the range of institutions represented by our membership had expanded to include seventy American and fourteen foreign institutions. For context, the number of institutions of higher education in America numbered about 1,000, so it's clear that the barriers remained in place. As such, the vast majority of members continued to come from a small minority of those colleges.

Over the years, there were some variations in the eligibility of candidates with graduate degrees who did not have an undergraduate degree. In every case, however, it was reiterated that a minimum number of years as an undergraduate in residence at an eligible institution was necessary. Eventually, it was determined that only undergraduate degrees would suffice (with the exception of some foreign graduate degrees that encompassed both undergraduate and graduate training and residency).

Access to higher education continued to grow (especially with the G.I. Bill), as did the number of colleges in America (more than 2,500 by 1970). Not surprisingly, the candidates being proposed for membership began to come from a dramatically broader array of universities and colleges. The detailed and extensive analysis of degrees and colleges became increasingly onerous for the Committee. While in the earlier years, the Committee's work resulted in the rejection of many colleges it reviewed, as the Club met in its second century, the Committee was generally recommending that most colleges be accepted. Indeed, by 1971, there were 350 American colleges and 60 foreign institutions on our eligible list. After much discussion and deliberation, it was decided in 1972 that the Club make eligible all colleges and degrees that had been accredited by the now well-established regional accreditation organizations.

Around this same time, there were interesting discussions on a more regular basis concerning non-residential college students and their eligibility. Candidates were being presented more regularly who had been night students or commuter students, i.e., they lived at home while pursuing their degrees. Extensive conversations with college administrators and alumni convinced the Committee that these students were enjoying an adequately robust undergraduate life and should be extended the opportunity to join the Club ranks. As such, the residency requirement was modified to reflect these new demographics, now requiring that candidates "attended" an eligible institution for at least three years. In the near future, with the dramatic increase in online education, the Club will need to determine once more what it means to attend an eligible institution.

The 1980s brought changes both small and large. The Committee on Admissions was given oversight of the Young Men's Club Activity Committee (now the Younger Members Committee) in its role in providing input in the review of younger candidates. More important, the Club opened its doors to women and the pool of candidates changed dramatically once again. The Committee on Admissions expanded its sights once more. The Club began its highly successful summer guest program, and the Committee on Admissions (itself now coed) took on the additional responsibility of hosting multiple receptions for summer candidates. This program more than doubled the number of candidates the Committee now interviewed each year.

As society and the Club have changed, so, too, has the Committee on Admissions adapted. While the Committee once considered only men from a small handful of institutions, today our membership includes men and women from about 600 colleges and universities located around the world. Despite the many changes within and without our walls, just as in the distant past, the twenty-one members of the Committee on Admissions may be found on the first Wednesday of each month in careful deliberation, striving to preserve the character of our cherished institution for the future.

A FINAL NOTE

"It is about a rather feeble brainchild, born just 75 years ago, at the close of the Civil War, a weakling at the start, but later waxing lusty and strong, until now, well past its three score years and ten, it is full of activity, respected, powerful and the parent of countless university clubs throughout the country."

—*Grosvenor Atterbury, Excerpt from talk given at the 75th anniversary dinner of The University Club, December 18, 1940*

The members who attended the dinner in 1940 would find much that is familiar to them in The University Club today, although they might be surprised by the absence of tobacco smoke. They would not recognize some parts of the clubhouse as they have been modified, and would certainly note that today's membership is drawn from a much wider section of the population than was the case seventy-five years ago. What has not changed is the members' commitment to literature and art, squash, backgammon and other games, good fellowship and fine dining in a convivial atmosphere.

A book such as this can only touch on highlights in covering a century and a half of activities. The authors hope that they have conveyed a sense of the vibrancy that has sustained the institution over the years. If the strength of the Club today is a precursor for the future, then when the bicentenary rolls around, Atterbury's words will still be apposite.

Percy Preston Jr.

One West 54th Street Foundation

Founded in 1999, the Foundation is an independent entity governed by a board of trustees who are completely separate from the Council of the Club. The Foundation is tax-exempt under Section 501(c)(3) of the Internal Revenue Code. Its mission is to enhance awareness of the landmark clubhouse, offer opportunities to future architects and, most important, to raise funds to maintain and restore the historic exterior of this magnificent building. To that end, Club members, other interested persons, and the Club itself may make contributions to the Foundation.

Over the years, the Foundation has contributed $5.1 million toward the restoration of the clubhouse. Among the projects supported in part with funds from the Foundation are repointing both the Fifth Avenue and 54th Street façades in compliance with Local Law 11, replacing most of the clubhouse windows, and installing the new glass canopy and doors at the main entrance. All of this work was done under the review of the New York City Landmarks Preservation Commission.

The Foundation also makes an annual gift to the Institute of Classical Architects.

• • • • • •

Charles F. McKim Society

The McKim Society is an informal recognition society sponsored by the Club. Individuals who give $5,000 or more to the One West 54th Street Foundation qualify for membership in the society. Today, there are 340 members. Each member receives a rosette to wear in his or her lapel. Every year, the Club hosts a festive event for McKim Society members in appreciation for their generosity.

PHOTO CREDITS & ACKNOWLEDGMENTS

Photographs not listed are from the collection of The University Club or are in the public domain.

Cover, pages 16, 18 (top right), 21 (top), 120, 125, 126, 127, 128 (top), 129, and 154, images on foldout 2 which follows page18: Jonathan Wallen Photography, Copyright © 2014, all rights reserved

Endpapers: William Walcot. *Entrance to The University Club*. Watercolor. 1922.

Page 2: Frank C. Bensing. *Theodore William Dwight, First President of The University Club*. Detail of oil on canvas portrait, after the original by Daniel Huntington

Page 3: Courtesy of the New York State Archives

Page 17: Ellen Emmet Rand. *Charles Follen McKim* (detail). Oil on canvas

View showing original roof garden: Courtesy of the Museum of the City of New York

Page 24: Kevin J. McCormack, Photographer

Page 29: IMG Licensing on behalf of Norman Rockwell

Page 31: Photographic print gift of Michael Weinberg

Page 37: Ellen Emmet Rand. *George Wickersham* (detail). Oil on canvas

Page 41: Courtesy of the Herbert Hoover Presidential Library-Museum

Page 73: Courtesy of the United States Military Academy

Pages 74 and 76: Photographic prints gift of Charles Scribner III

Page 79: All courtesy of the Municipal Archives of the City of New York

Page 83: Copyright © The Richard Avedon Foundation

Page 111: Ted Turner, copyright © Cable News Network, Inc.

Former President Carter, courtesy of the Jimmy Carter Presidential Library

Former President Nixon, collection of The University Club

Barbara Walters, © Donna Svennevik/American Broadcasting Companies, Inc.

Page 113: Opie / New Yorker Collection / www.cartoonbank.com

Page 115: Collection of the Supreme Court of the United States

Page 116: Photograph of Walter Isaacson by Patrice Gilbert

Book jacket photograph of Steve Jobs by Albert Watson

Page 117: Photograph of Jon Meacham by Gasper Tingale

Page 121: Ellen Emmett Rand. *Henry Holt* (detail). Oil on canvas.

Page 122: Irving Ramsey Wiles. *A. Barton Hepburn* (detail). Oil on canvas

Page 125: Photograph of group by Athlyn Fitz-James

Pages 134–143: All photographs by Timothy R. Hamilton, except Stanford White (collection of The University Club) and figure 22, courtesy of the Caldwell archive

Page 146: Top: Ralph Morse / The LIFE Picture Collection / Getty Images

Bottom and photographs on page 147 provided by Peter Otto

Page 163: Photograph by Alex Conti

Page 165: Photographs by Percy Preston Jr.

Pages 169–170: Photographs by Jonathan Raible